If I
Killed
a Deer

If I Killed a Deer
Copyright © 2010 Richard Ellett Mullin

ISBN-10: 0-9846003-0-2
ISBN-13: 978-0-9846003-0-4

formatting /design by
Rend Graphics
www.rendgraphics.com

Published by Provendre

If I
Killed
a Deer

Venison Recipes, Food Trivia & Musings
of a
Carolina Hunter & Cook

Richard Ellett Mullin
Charleston, South Carolina

CONTENTS

Slow Cooked Venison-Southern Style

Slow Cooked Venison-International

Fast Cooked Venison

Ground Venison

Venison Sausages

Venison Soups

Salads

 # Vegetable Side Dishes

 # Starch Side Dishes
(Rice, Potatoes & Corn)

Pickles and Conserves

Desserts

Venison
Food Fit for a King

This cookbook is dedicated to Gaston Phoebus, Lord of the Pyrenees, Count of Foix 1331-1391 who wrote: "Tout mon temps me suis délité par espicial en trois choses, l'une est en armes, l'autre est en amours, et l'autre si est en chasse...I have always especially delighted in three things: one is fighting, the other is love, and the last is the hunt".

Tens of thousands of years before Phoebus, men painted vivid scenes of hunting large game on the walls of caves in both Spain and France, not far from the domain of Phoebus on both sides of the Pyrenees.

In Roman mythology, Diana the virginal goddess of the hunt was associated with oak groves, moonlight, and fertility, three things that are very familiar to any modern day deer hunter! The Temple at Ephesus was dedicated to Diana, and for 3 years Ephesus became the home base for Paul of Tarsus, whose letter to the Ephesians included the memorable words, "For it is by grace that you have been saved through faith, and this is not your own doing, it is the gift of God". Fifteen hundred years later the Protestant Reformation was born of those words.

Before the rein of Charlemagne people hunted mostly for subsistence in Europe, and it was practiced by peasant and patrician alike. Hunting in the Middle Ages became the passion and occupation of nobles, and it was glorified in books including the Livre de la Chasse by our own Gaston Phoebus. An anonymous book, Chasse de la Cerf details the running of deer with hounds. So tradition was born, and it lives on today in the running of deer with hounds in the Lowcountry, complete with a mounted huntmaster and drivers riding "marsh tackies".

Medieval custom even governed how the deer's carcass was divided up among participants: the hunter, the noble landowner, the warden, etc. The skin went to the man who killed the deer, the loin to the huntsman who butchered or "broke" the animal, the right shoulder to the Parson, a quarter to poor men, the left shoulder to the forester, etc., etc.

So strict were the rules of the hunt that infractions in game laws exposed the perpetrator to harsh penalties including blinding or castration. Those are powerful deterrents to trespassers!

Here are recipes reflecting my own love of cooking venison. Enjoy.

Venison
in South Carolina

About 1989 I met a fellow named John Riley in Charlotte. John ran a concrete plant there. He was from Cross, SC, and he had guided for striped bass on Lake Moultrie at one time. I will never forget his bellowing description of the Lowcountry's deer season, "August to January, shoot all you want, no limit". That pretty well summarizes it.

I fished with John Riley a number of times, and we always went with guide June English out of Black's Landing on Lake Moultrie. This was when Russell Blackmon who owned Black's Landing was still alive. Russell was reputed to be a direct descendent of Francis Marion, the Swamp Fox. When you entered the restaurant at Black's there was a diorama on one wall, with a life-sized painting of Francis Marion on horseback surrounded by his men. In the foreground were several stuffed deer including a piebald doe. However if you looked closely, the Swamp Fox was not Francis Marion at all; it was a short framed man with Russell Blackmon's face. It pleased John Riley to no end to point this out to a first time visitor as he hooted "Russell is the ugliest man on earth!"

In the winter of 2006-2007 a Charleston friend took a group of us on a duck hunting trip on a private impoundment near Rimini on the upper end of Lake Marion. This was was one well planned trip! The night we arrived we had an oyster roast as an appetizer. Then we moved indoors and feasted Lowcountry style. Among the things served was the Lowcountry classic Mustard Fried Venison (Pg. 55). If there is a signature dish for South Carolina venison, Mustard Fried Venison has to be that dish.

Years before, in 1981 my first job out of college was as an engineer with Schlumberger Offshore Services based in Morgan City, Louisiana. It was a rare offshore oil rig that didn't serve "Chicken-Fried Steak" at least one meal a day. I can't help but think of those days because the "Chicken Fried Steak" we ate so often on those oil rigs was hauntingly similar to South Carolina's beloved Mustard Fried Venison!

South Carolina hunters kill an average of 225,000 deer a year out of an estimated herd of 750,000. That's about 5% of the annual U.S. harvest of 5,000,000 deer per year. The South Carolina Dept. of Natural Resources website says, "you have a better chance of being struck by lightning than shooting a Boone & Crockett buck", so hunt 'em for meat!

Guide to Cuts of Venison

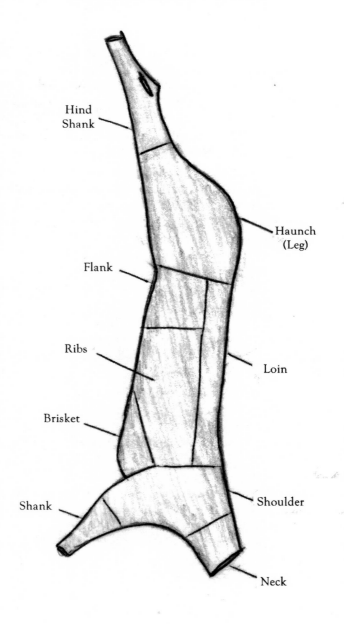

Hind Shank

Haunch (Leg)

Flank

Ribs

Loin

Brisket

Shank

Shoulder

Neck

Notes on Cuts of Venison

If your deer processor is giving you a cooler full of burger, cube-steak and a couple of boneless loins, you will miss out on a lot of these recipes. Consider asking your butcher to give you back a variety of cuts:

(1) the fat ribs,

(2) the neck roast,

(3) the shanks from your deer (and from your hunting buddy's deer!).

(4) the flank meat from both sides of the animal.

Flank can be rolled and tied for a rolled roast, tenderized for rouladen, or it is good to use to make home-made corned venison. Otherwise the flank and the rib meat will end up in the form of burger. Regarding burger, the norm among venison processors in our area is about 15% added beef fat.

(5) I ask for only 10% beef fat to be added to my venison burger.

(6) Request a lot of large stew chunks (2"), and boneless roasts.

(7) Finally, take the liver and heart home that day, and use fresh.

Packaging bone-in cuts takes up more plastic vacuum bag space, and more room in the freezer, so I still favor a majority of boneless cuts for convenience. But for a party sized bone-in roast, see the Heribert Von Feilizsch's Whole Roast Venison Loin recipe in this book!

The ribs should ideally not be stored for long periods in the freezer since they do have a relatively high component of fat, and venison fat is susceptible to turning rancid fairly quickly. However, vacuum packing works magic, and nothing beats barbequed venison ribs with their succulent fat and all! Ribs are often the first cut I cook after getting a deer back from the processor.

It's your choice, but consider providing more input into how your animal is butchered. If you want to enjoy a variety of venison recipes you need a variety of cuts! Xerox this page, circle what you want on the 7 items above, and leave it with your butcher the next time you kill a deer.

Finally, check out the U-Tube video titled "Roe Deer Butchering" at "TheHuntingLife.com" for a good tutorial on breaking down a deer. Good luck understanding this British butcher's accent! He is a master with the knife, proving you don't have to saw bone to break down a deer.

Slow Cooked Venison
Southern Style

Venison Gombo
Braised Venison with Okra

With the South Carolina deer season starting during the middle of August, it is not just likely, but absolutely assured that okra will be available when the first deer of the season are killed.

Ingredients:

2 lbs. venison cut into large stew chunks or steaks

4 - 5 tbsp. olive oil

2 onions chopped fine

3 strips of thick market bacon diced (dry cured if possible)

4 carrots peeled and diced (optional)

2 bay leaves

½ tsp. dried thyme

3 cloves garlic chopped

Handful of parsley chopped

1 cup red wine

Half pound (or more) fresh okra sliced in rounds or whole pods

4 peeled tomatoes chopped

Salt & fresh ground black pepper to taste

Directions:

Heat half the olive oil in a fry pan or Dutch oven. Brown the meat on all sides then remove to a separate bowl. Add the rest of the olive oil and sauté' onions and bacon for 10 minutes until the onions begin to turn golden. Add the carrots if using. Put the meat on top of the layer of veggies in the Dutch oven or Crockpot. Sprinkle with herbs, salt and pepper. Don't over salt because the bacon will contribute some salt and the pan juices will reduce and concentrate at the end of cooking.

Add the wine, or if using a Crockpot, deglaze the fry pan with the wine & then add it to Crockpot. Scatter the okra and tomatoes on top. Bring to a good simmer. Put on the lid and cook for about 1 ½ to 2 hours. Remove the lid and finish cooking in the oven on 350 degrees for another 15-20 minutes to reduce the pan juices if desired. Serve with rice, bread, pasta, or potatoes.

Venison Steaks
in Dill Pickle & Onion Gravy

We went on a trip to New York to celebrate my wife's 50th birthday. While she did some antique buying for her business, I tagged along looking at books everywhere we went. Among my purchases was one called **The Russian Heritage Cookbook** *by Lynn Visson. Several of her beef recipes lend themselves to use with venison. This one combines venison steaks with smoky bacon, onion and sour dill pickles for a dish reminiscent of the German dish rouladen without as much work.*

Ingredients:

1 ½ lbs. venison steaks sliced about ½" - ¾" thick

Flour for dredging the meat

3 strips smoky thick cut market bacon

1 medium onion sliced into thin slices

1 large sour dill pickle or 2 - 3 small dill pickled cucumbers

1 ½ cups beef, chicken, or venison broth

½ tsp. very coarsely ground black pepper

1 tsp. salt

1 ½ tbsp. butter

Sour cream (opt.)

Handful fresh minced parsley

Directions:

Salt and pepper the steaks, and dredge in flour, shaking off the excess. In a large skillet or Dutch oven, sauté bacon until cooked. Drain and add butter. Brown steaks on medium high in the butter. Remove the steaks to a plate. Add onions to the pan, & sauté until transparent. Next add minced dill pickle and stir. Scrape onions and pickles to the side. and return the steaks to the pan making a single layer on the bottom of the pan. Spoon the onion and pickle mix over the steaks, and add the broth, bringing everything up to a simmer on medium heat.

Cover, and simmer for about 1 ½ hours on low heat. Check occasionally to prevent burning, and add a little water from time to time to make sure the dish does not dry out and burn. It is ok to let the gravy reduce down several times and to re-constitute it with water. This actually helps tenderize the meat. When the meat is tender, serve a piece of steak on each plate with some gravy, and place a tablespoon full of sour cream on top of each serving and a little minced parsley if desired. Good with boiled potatoes.

Venison Rouladen
with Pickled Okra

This recipe is of German descent. Typically it is based on using an inexpensive beef round steak pounded thin, and rolled around a dill pickle spear. Rouladen is known in Louisiana, but not in South Carolina. My Lowcountry version uses venison cube steak wrapped around a pod of pickled okra. You can still use dill pickle if you don't have access to any pickled okra! Try this dish served with egg noodles or boiled potatoes and a glass of red wine or beer.

Ingredients:

2 lb. venison cube steaks or steaks tenderized with mallet

6 - 8 pickled okra pods, drained

1 med. onion chopped fine

Strips of thick smoked market bacon (cut in 2 equal halves)

Flour for dusting (rice or wheat)

Prepared mustard (spicy brown or Dijon)

1 cup red wine or 12 oz bottle of beer or ale

Salt & fresh ground black pepper to taste

1 - 2 tbsp. Worcestershire sauce

Directions:

Lay the tenderized steaks out flat. Spread 1 tsp. mustard on the top of each steak. Salt and pepper to taste. Next put a pickled okra pod on each steak, and begin to roll the steak around the okra pod. When you have about 1" to 1 ½" of meat left to roll, then lay a piece of bacon down on the middle of the steak, and continue rolling to secure the end of the bacon inside of the roulade. Continue rolling the bacon around the roulade, wrapping it tightly, and then secure the roll with a toothpick or kitchen twine. Continue to make rolls out of all of the steaks and pickled okra pods.

In a fry pan, brown a couple strips of the bacon. Remove most of the bacon grease and reserve. Add the chopped onion to the pan. Cook the onion until translucent, continuing cooking and caramelizing the onions until reduced and browned nicely. Remove the onions from the pan.

Add a couple of tablespoons of the bacon grease back to the pan, and put the meat rolls in the pan and brown the meat rolls on all sides. After removing the meat, sprinkle 2 tbsp. flour in the bottom of the fry pan, and add a little more bacon grease if needed. Then brown the flour in the remaining oil, making a roux about the color of a brown paper bag.

Transfer the onions and bacon, and the browned meat rolls into the pan. Add the wine, beer, or ale, and season with Worcestershire sauce, salt and black pepper, and put on the lid. Note, if your okra is hot pickled okra great. If not, you may want to add a pinch of cayenne pepper or red pepper flakes to the pot prior to putting on the lid to simmer for about 1¼ hours depending on how tender the meat is.

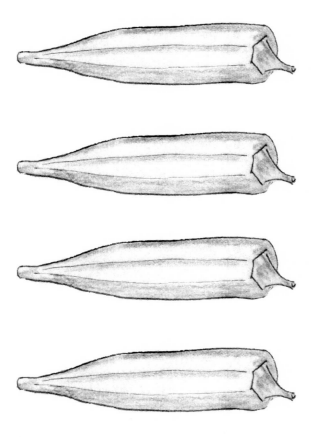

Country Style Venison
with Caramelized Onion & Eggplant Gravy

My daughter Stafford and I bought 2 Japanese "Ichiban" eggplant seedlings at Lowes in late May, 2009. We planted them in some of Jay Steele's compost he makes up at the Tri-County Cotton Gin near Kingstree. There we planted them, right next to our front gate columns on Gibbes Street in downtown Charleston. Immediately the plants took off, One became a large shrub, and ended up producing nearly a bushel of beautiful long glossy eggplants, which we cooked in various ways over the course of the summer. Late in August I had been watching half a dozen eggplants mature, and late one afternoon I noticed they were gone. Stafford and I traded theories on the thief, but lo to our surprise the next day, my good friend Chris Keach confessed to taking them home for supper, and the mystery was solved. This is a recipe I came up with as a result of our eggplant embarrassment of riches, using some venison steaks from the freezer.

Ingredients:

1 ½ lbs. venison cube steak or other thin steaks

Flour

4 - 5 tbsp. olive oil

2 large onions chopped

1 lg. eggplant (peel & dice) or 2 - 3 Japanese eggplants (dice)

1 large tomato peeled and chopped

1 bay leaf

1 tsp. sweet paprika

Few flakes cayenne pepper

1 clove garlic peeled & coarsely chopped

1 cup water

Salt & fresh ground black pepper to taste

Directions:

Salt and pepper the steaks, and dredge in flour (rice flour if gluten intolerant). Shake off the excess flour. In a large fry pan, using half of the oil, brown the meat on both sides and remove from the pan and set aside on a plate. Then add the rest of the oil, and the onions and cook them until translucent. Continue to reduce the onions until they begin to caramelize, then remove them from the pan and set aside. Add a little more oil, and add the diced eggplant, and cook until wilted. Add the paprika, garlic, and tomato, and stir.

Next, recombine the steak, onion, and all of the seasonings in the pan with the eggplant mixture. Add 1 cup water, and bring up to a hard simmer, and cook covered to thicken the gravy. Depending on how tender the meat is, cook for about 1 hour. Monitor to prevent burning, but allow enough heat for the gravy to reduce down several times, thus further caramelizing the onions and eggplant. Add ½ cup water each time, and re-cover, continuing to simmer briskly. You should have a nice brown thick gravy at the end, with lots of concentrated flavors. Serve with plain rice or pasta.

Cola Barbequed Venison Ribs

This sauce and dry rub is something my daughter Stafford learned about on the Food Network website. It is a recipe posted there by The Neeleys. It is great with pork ribs, but equally good using venison ribs if you adjust the sweetness by using less sugar than called for. The first time we made this, Stafford and I doubled the sauce recipe, and put some up in a Mason jar to use later to save us some time when we wanted ribs again. Plan to double these sauce & dry rub recipes and put the extra up in a jars. Then later you can use them to make the S.C. Masterpiece BBQ Venison Meatloaf (Pg. 74). The Neeleys cook their ribs on the grill. Venison takes longer to cook than pork, and needs more moisture, so we pan roast them in the oven.

Ingredients Neeleys Sauce:

1 tbsp. vegetable oil

1 onion finely minced

3 cloves garlic minced finely

2 cups tomato ketchup

1 can or bottle Coca-Cola or Pepsi (12 oz.- not diet)

½ cup apple cider vinegar

2 tbsp. brown sugar (delete for sauce for venison ribs)

½ tbsp. fresh ground black pepper

½ tbsp. onion powder

½ tbsp. dry mustard

Juice of a lemon

1 tbsp. Worcestershire Sauce

Neeleys Sauce Directions:

Heat the oil in a saucepan and sauté the onion and garlic until transparent. Add all of the other ingredients and cook uncovered. Stir frequently, and simmer for about 1 hour to reduce and thicken.

Ingredients Neeleys Dry Rub:

2 tbsp. salt

2 tbsp. brown sugar (reduce to 1 tbsp. for venison ribs)

2 tsp. garlic powder

2 tsp. onion powder

1 tsp. cumin

1 tsp. chili powder

1 tsp. fresh ground black pepper

Dry Rub Directions:

Put all of the ingredients in a jar with a tight fitting lid and shake to blend. Make some extra and store the jar in the refrigerator for later use.

The Ribs:

Season the ribs on both sides with dry rub. Place the ribs in a zip lock bag and refrigerate overnight. Use as many ribs as you want to prepare, and will fit in your cooking pan in a single layer. I use a long rectangular Pyrex baking dish about 2" deep.

Cooking Directions:

Take the ribs out of the zip lock bag and arrange them in the Pyrex baking dish. Pour 3 - 4 tbsp. cooking oil over the ribs. Slice a medium onion and scatter the slices over the meat. Place the pan in a slow oven (about 250 degrees). Cook for about 2½ hours covered with an aluminum foil tent loosely placed over the ribs so they don't dry out. Check mid way to make sure the meat is not drying out.

Next, remove the foil tent, and cover the ribs with the cola barbeque sauce using an amount adequate to cover them.

Return to the oven for another hour on 250 degrees. Raise the oven temperature to 350 degrees for the last 15 minutes to finish them off brown, and to reduce the sauce if it is thin. Serve with potato salad.

Jamaican Style Venison Curry
with Johns Island Pumpkin

This is a Caribbean inspired recipe frequently used for goat meat.

Based on the way the deer eat anything within their reach on my farm in Williamsburg County, deer are our wild equivalent of goats. They will eat almost anything. Here's a recipe to treat them like a goat!

Sidi Limehouse who has Rosebank Farms on Johns Island grows an amazing variety of pumpkins & hard squash. I bought a little calabaza from him and turned out some fine curry like this to spoon over my rice.

The presence of allspice makes this distinctly Jamaican in flavor. No allspice, no Jamaica. In fact the word "jamaica" is the word for allspice in Spanish, although it is called "pimento" in Jamaica. About the year 1500 it excited the Spanish to find this exotic spice growing there.

Jamaican Curry Powder Ingredients (grind in spice grinder):

5 teaspoons ground turmeric

4 teaspoons coriander seeds

3 teaspoons cayenne pepper

3 teaspoons fenugreek seeds

2 teaspoons cumin seeds

2 teaspoons whole black pepper

2 teaspoons star anise or ground cinnamon

2 teaspoons yellow mustard seeds

1 whole clove

1 teaspoon ground ginger

1 teaspoon grated nutmeg

1 teaspoon whole allspice.

Ingredients:

1½ lb. venison stew cut into 1" cubes

1 lb. peeled calabaza, pumpkin, or butternut squash, 1" cubes

1 fresh pepper (green, red, banana, hot or sweet)

1 onion peeled and chopped

2 garlic cloves minced

3 tbsp. cooking oil

1½ tbsp. "Grace" Jamaican curry powder (or subst. using recipe above)

2 bay leaves

2 tomatoes peeled and chopped

2 tbsp. tomato paste

1 cup water plus water added at intervals to prevent sticking

1 cup coconut milk to finish (optional)

2 tbsp. butter

1 lime, quartered

Directions:

Put the meat in a Ziploc bag, and sprinkle with the 1½ tbsp. curry powder. Place in the refrigerator overnight. Heat the oil in a non-stick skillet and as soon as it is hot, put in the bay leaves. As quick as they begin to turn brown (a few seconds) quickly put in the meat and brown it on all sides. Remove meat to a plate.

Next add the onions, garlic and peppers to the pan, and sauté for a few minutes. Follow by adding the tomatoes and the tomato paste along with the water (and coconut milk if using) and the pumpkin or squash. Bring to a simmer in the skillet, add meat, and cover. This curry can be transferred to the Crockpot and simmered at this point if you desire.

For tender cuts of venison, cook the curry about 45 minutes until the pumpkin and meat are tender. Note, if you have tough cuts of stew meat you want to cook it for 30-40 minutes before adding the pumpkin. This prevents having the pumpkin falling apart while the meat is still tough. In this case, cook all ingredients another 25-30 minutes after adding the pumpkin. Add a little water along the way if the sauce reduces down and is in danger of sticking. 5 minutes before serving the curry, finish by adding the butter, stir to blend, heat through, and serve with white rice.

Give everybody a quarter of a lime on their plate to squeeze a little juice over the curry to give it that last bit of zing!

Roast Venison
in Tomatoes, Lemon, & Muscadine Wine

I'm not much on drinking Muscadine wine, but it is great for cooking. In North Carolina where I grew up we called it Scuppernong wine. Or if you run into someone really country, they call it Scupperdine wine! I began making it out of wild picked grapes when I was about 10 years old, and ever since, I never have lost the bug for making wine. Muscadine wine is made from the Vitis Rotundifolia grape which has a round leaf, and a thick slip skin on the berry. The variety is resistant to Pierce's Disease, Phylloxera, and the many funguses we have in our humid climate. So the Muscadine grape is one of the only grapes that will flourish in the Southern Coastal Plain. Around Charleston, Irvin House Vineyard on Wadmalaw Island makes Muscadine wine.

Ingredients:

3 to 4 lb. venison roast

4 tbsp. olive oil, cooking oil, or lard

1 lemon seeded and cut into 8 wedges

4 cloves garlic chopped coarsely

1 can chopped tomatoes (15 oz.)

2 cups red Muscadine wine

1 ½ tsp. salt or to taste

1 cinnamon stick

½ tsp. fresh ground black pepper

1 tsp. dried thyme leaves

Directions:

Use half of the salt and pepper on the roast and rub on the outside with 1 tbsp. of the oil. Put the rest of the oil in a large frying pan or heavy bottomed Dutch oven. Quickly brown the roast on all sides on medium high heat, then remove the roast from the pan and hold it on a plate or transfer it to a Crockpot.

Place the lemon wedges (including the peel) in the pan, mash with a spatula, and stir to deglaze the bottom of the pan. Next add the garlic, tomatoes, thyme, cinnamon stick, and the rest of the salt and pepper. Raise the heat to bring the contents of the pan to a boil. Add the 2 cups of wine, and heat it until everything begins to simmer, then transfer the hot mixture to the Crockpot, pouring it over the roast. If using a Dutch oven, transfer the roast back into the Dutch oven and settle it down in the liquid.

Cook the roast for 3-4 hours in the Crockpot on the high setting, or until it is completely tender. If using a Dutch oven, place it in the oven on 300 degrees and cook for 2 hours. If using a large roast (like an entire leg of venison) adjust the ingredient amounts and cooking time accordingly. This is not to be done as a rare roast. It should be tender as a result of slow braising in the liquid.

After the roast is done, remove it from the Crockpot or Dutch oven and put it on a serving platter to rest. Meanwhile, pour the tomato-lemon-wine pot liquor into a large saucepan, and heat it on the stove top on high. Reduce the sauce down to half in volume, then pour the reduced sauce over the roast, and serve immediately.

Crockpot Stew of Venison
with Ripe Bell Peppers

For this recipe, use ripe red sweet bell peppers, or if available, the yellow and orange peppers for a combination of colors. Green bell peppers are not as sweet and flavorful. Use them only as a last resort.

Ingredients:

2 lb. venison stew meat in large chunks (1½" to 2")

2 sweet ripe bell peppers seeded & chopped coarsely

1 large onion-chopped

2 large cloves garlic minced

¼ tsp. cayenne pepper flakes

½ tsp. dried thyme

2 large tomatoes peeled and chopped coarsely

3 - 4 tbsp. olive oil

½ cup red or white table wine

1 tsp. salt

½ tsp. fresh ground black pepper

Directions:

Put meat in a covered bowl or Ziploc bag with the wine, salt, garlic, black pepper, thyme and pepper flakes, and refrigerate overnight. Turn it several times to make sure the spices are evenly distributed. When you are ready to cook the dish, drain the meat completely through a sieve, and reserve the marinade along with the spices it contains. When the meat is drained dry it is ready to brown.

In a large nonstick skillet, pour half of the oil, and heat on med-high. Add the meat and brown it on all sides, then transfer it to the Crockpot.

Next, add the rest of the oil to the fry pan along with the onions and sauté until they are wilted, about 5 minutes. Add the pepper slices and continue to cook these together until the onions are lightly browned and peppers are softened. Transfer onions and peppers to the Crockpot.

Deglaze skillet with the reserved wine marinade, making sure to include all of the spices it contains. Place the chopped tomato in the boiling pan juices, and as soon as it boils again, scrape the pan with a spatula to get all of the pan juices, and pour the entire contents into the Crockpot. Place the lid on the Crockpot and cook on high for about 2 hours. Or cook on low all day, or as long as needed for the meat to become tender.

Venison Pot Roast
a` la Budweiser

Ingredients:

2 - 3 lbs. venison roast

2 - 3 tbsp. cooking oil

2 strips bacon

1 lg. onion peeled and chopped medium

2 carrots peeled and chopped

1 large celery rib chopped

1 can beer (12 oz.)

1 bay leaf

Handful of chopped fresh parsley

½ tsp. very coarsely ground black pepper

1 tsp. salt

Directions:

Salt and pepper the roast, and brown it on all sides in the oil in a deep Dutch oven or skillet about 10 - 15 minutes. Remove the roast from the pan and hold on a plate or if using a Crockpot, place it in the Crockpot set on low.

Add the vegetables to the pan, and sauté the onion, celery, and carrots for about 10 minutes until the vegetables are wilted. Return the meat to the pan, and lay the two strips of bacon over the top of the roast. Then add the beer, and cover. Place in the oven to bake for about 2 hours on 325 degrees, or until tender.

If using the Crockpot, place the roast in the Crockpot, then lay the bacon strips on top of the roast, and pour the hot vegetables around the roast, add the beer, and put the lid on. Cook all day on low, or cook for about 2½ to 3 hours in the Crockpot on high.

Crockpot Sabbath Stew
of Venison & Sieva Beans

The year 1492 was an eventful one for Ferdinand and Isabella of Spain. Their hired Genoan sailor named Columbus was "discovering" the new world. The same year all Jews remaining on the Iberian Peninsula who had not heeded the command to convert to Catholicism were evicted. Bean cookery, especially in one pot stews prepared in advance of the Sabbath had reached an art form among the Sephardim (Jews of Spain, Portugal, and Morocco). Folks saw eating beans as an indication of your being Jewish, and anyone caught eating Jewish fare was liable to find himself in a hot place with the Inquisition, if you know what I mean. So conversos and the general populace began using pork in these stews in defiance of Jewish dietary law as a way of demonstrating that they were Christian. So today, many Spanish bean dishes use pork. Instead of beans, it is pork itself that has been elevated to an art form there.

Originally bean dishes in Europe used the old world fava bean. Beans as we know them came from the New World. This dish is a rustic stew that calls for dried Lima beans. Around Charleston a Lima bean is known as a Sieva bean (Phaseolus Lunatus which translates literally as "moon shaped bean"). Thought to have originated in Guatemala originally, there are over 100 named varieties of Lima beans in all colors and sizes and shapes. Several kinds of dried Lima beans are available through Hayes Foods of Greenville, SC under their "Star" brand, including Speckled Butterbeans (dark black and brown in color), Large White Limas, and Baby Green Butterbeans.

This recipe is true to the original Jewish dietary law when using venison. Since both the deer and the steer part the hoof and chew the cud, they are considered clean. In fact there were a number of Jews who came to Charleston early in the life of the Carolina colony. So many that Charleston and its vicinity had more Jews than anywhere in the American Colonies by the year 1800. This recipe is just a little something to remind us of South Carolina's part in the Diaspora while doing it with our local ingredients.

Note the addition of whole eggs that are cooked in the stew. These are known as "huevos haminados". Alone, eggs for sabbath consumption may be cooked for long periods in coffee grounds and onion skins to obtain a deep stained color. Traditionally the stew would have been divided at service, and the meat, beans, and eggs served as separate dishes.

Ingredients:

1½ lb. stew venison cut into 1" chunks

1 cup dried Lima (Sieva) beans soaked overnight

1 onion, chopped

2 cloves garlic minced

4 tbsp. olive oil

2 tbsp. honey

1½ tsp. paprika

½ tsp. fresh ground black pepper

½ tsp. ground cumin

½ tsp. ground cinnamon

¼ tsp. ground turmeric or pinch of saffron threads crumbled

1½ tsp. salt

4 - 6 whole unbroken brown shelled eggs

4 - 6 cups of vegetable, chicken, venison, or beef broth

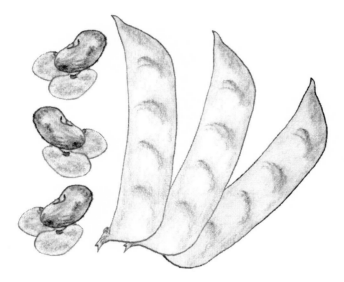

Directions:

Soak beans overnight covered in water. Drain beans when ready to assemble this dish. Take eggs out of the fridge and allow to come to room temperature. Turn Crockpot on low. Heat oil in large nonstick skillet. Add onions and sauté until transparent. Transfer to the crock pot. Add meat to the pan and brown on all sides, then put in the garlic, spices and honey. Heat through, then transfer over to the Crockpot. Next put the beans in the skillet and cover with broth. Bring to a boil then transfer the beans and liquid to the Crockpot. Rinse eggs and nestle them gently down in the stew evenly spaced around in the Crockpot. Put the lid on and cook overnight on low. Serve the next day for Sabbath lunch.

Caffeine Lovers' Venison
Stew, Roast or Ribs

Coleman Andrews has a recipe called "Estofat de Bou" in his book **Catalan Cuisine***. It is a beef stew that uses chocolate. This recipe goes one step further for rich brown gravy lovers. I have heard that anyone whose astrological sign is Capricorn is a lover of savory brown gravies and sauces. Having been born in January, it certainly is true in my case. Of course "capri" means goats, and goats will eat anything!*

Ingredients:
2 - 3 lbs. venison roast (or stew meat or ribs)

3 - 4 tbsp. cooking oil or lard

1 cup strong left-over black coffee

2 oz. dark chocolate

2 - 3 large cloves garlic mashed and minced

1 lg. onion peeled and chopped

3 - 4 potatoes peeled and quartered

½ tsp. dried thyme leaves

½ tsp. very coarsely ground black pepper

1½ tsp. salt or to taste

2 - 3 tbsp. softened butter with 1 tbsp. flour mashed together

Directions:
Salt and pepper meat, and brown on all sides in the oil in a large frying pan or Dutch oven. If using a crock pot, remove the roast (or ribs) to the crock pot. If baking it, remove the roast to a plate temporarily.

Sautee chopped onions & garlic in the frying pan or Dutch oven until wilted and beginning to brown. Add coffee, chocolate, and thyme, & bring to boil. Pour the hot mixture over the meat in the Crockpot, or if using a Dutch oven, return the roast to the Dutch oven and settle it down in the coffee gravy. Cook all day in the crock pot on low, or 3 hours on high. If roasting in oven, cook for about 1-½ - 2 hours on 325 degrees. Add potatoes near the end and cook them with the roast until tender.

Remove the roast to a serving plate. Pour the cooking broth into a large saucepan set on the eye of the stove. Boil to reduce it by about 50%. Finally, add the butter-flour mixture at the end to the boiling broth to thicken it. Pour thickened gravy over the roast and potatoes and serve.

Slow Cooked Venison
International

If I Killed a Deer

Cervo Cacciatore
Italian Hunter's Venison

This is a nice recipe for slow cooking venison with mushrooms for a hearty dish. The tomatoes certainly mark it as Italian.

Ingredients:

2 - 3 lbs. venison roast or stew chunks

1 lg. onion peeled and chopped medium

1 lb. fresh mushrooms (white or baby portabella)

1 large celery rib chopped

2 - 3 large garlic cloves minced

1 cup red table wine

1 can tomato sauce or crushed tomatoes (15 oz. can)

2 tbsp. tomato paste

3 - 4 tbsp. olive oil

1 bay leaf

Handful of chopped fresh parsley

½ tsp. dried thyme leaves

½ tsp. very coarsely ground black pepper

1 tsp. salt

Directions:

Salt and pepper the meat, and brown on all sides in the oil in a Dutch oven or skillet. Remove meat from the pan and hold on a plate or if using a Crockpot, place it in the Crockpot set on low. Add a little more oil, and sauté the onion, celery, & mushrooms until the vegetables are wilted. Add tomato sauce or crushed tomatoes, tomato paste, all of the seasonings, and wine, and bring the ingredients to a simmer over medium high heat. If using the Crockpot, pour the hot vegetables and sauce over the meat, and put the lid on. Cook all day on low, or cook for about 2 - 2½ hours in the Crockpot on high. If cooking in the oven, return meat to the pan, cover with a lid or foil, and roast on 300 degrees for about 2 hours, or until tender. If thicker sauce is desired, remove the meat from the pan and place the pan on the stove top. Stir constantly while heating over medium high heat to reduce the sauce by half. Pour the tomato-mushroom sauce over the meat. Serve with polenta and some grated Parmigiano cheese.

Gambe di Cervo
Italian Style Braised Venison Shanks

Gambe means shank, and cervo means deer in Italian. This is based on the classic Osso Buco which traditionally uses veal shanks. Plan to cook the venison shanks for a long time to insure they are so tender the meat falls off the bone. Long slow cooking is needed to break down all of the connective tissue when cooking any shanks like this. Using the crock pot achieves this with low energy usage. The three steps are (1) brown and sauté, (2) slow cooking in the crock pot, and (3) finish in oven to reduce & thicken the sauce as needed. This 3 step procedure is a good model for lots of venison recipes.

Braised shanks are traditionally served in Italy with a yellow starch for striking color contrast on the plate. Milanese-style would be influenced by the rice growing region of the Po River and it would be served with a nice saffron risotto (Risotto Milanese). Meanwhile, In Tuscany and Umbria you might expect to find the dominant grain being yellow corn in the form of polenta. This is the characteristic grain of their poverty kitchen. Poverty fare! Calling this poverty fare is exactly the opposite of what it is, rich & elegant!

Ingredients:

2 - 3 lbs. venison shanks cut into 1½" thick slices on meat saw

Flour for dusting

4 - 5 tbsp. olive oil

4 - 5 tbsp. butter

1 lg. onion chopped fine

½ cup celery finely chopped

½ cup carrots finely chopped

¼ cup chopped parsley

3 tbsp. tomato paste

½ cup Port or Marsala wine

2 lg. cloves garlic peeled & finely chopped

1 bay leaf

½ tsp. dried thyme leaves or one fresh sprig

2 cups prepared chicken or beef broth

½ tsp. black pepper

1 tsp. salt

Directions:

Season meat with salt and pepper & dredge the shanks in flour and shake off all of the excess. Heat half of the olive oil and butter in a large non-stick skillet. Brown the meat on all sides on medium high heat, making sure you have room in the pan for each shank, to prevent the meat from cooking slowly and releasing its moisture. We want it to brown, not boil! Remove the meat from the skillet and put in the bottom of a large Crockpot.

Add the rest of the oil and butter to the skillet, and put the onion, carrots, and celery in to sauté. Continue to cook, stirring on medium, until the onions are beginning to caramelize. Browning the onions and other vegetables will impart sweetness and color to the finished sauce. Remove the browned vegetables from the skillet, and put them in the Crockpot with the browned shanks.

De-glaze the skillet with the wine on medium high, and once steaming, add tomato paste, salt, pepper, bay leaf, thyme, garlic, and the broth. Heat the liquid mixture through to boiling. Transfer the hot liquid over into the Crockpot, and put the top on. Cook on the low heat setting on the Crockpot for as many hours as you can stand the delicious smell. Ideally plan to start this in the early morning, and come home to it for supper. Or start at night, and serve it the next day for lunch.

About an hour before meal time take off the lid, and put the Crockpot on high to cook for an hour uncovered to thicken and reduce the sauce. If your slow cooker won't heat up adequately. Remove shanks & pop the crock in the oven and bake on 375 degrees for 20 - 30 minutes to reduce the sauce so it is thick and sticks to shanks when you return them to the sauce. Plate the shanks with some Risotto Milanese (pg. 123) or polenta (pg. 126). Sprinkle the cooked shanks with gremolata if desired.

Gremolata:

Peel a lemon and and orange. Lay the peel strips on a cutting board, and slice the white lining off, leaving only the orange and yellow peel portions. Place in a small food chopper, or grate finely. Put 2 cloves raw garlic and 2 tbsp. parsley in the food chopper also. Process just long enough by pulsing to mince all of the ingredients finely. Use as garnish on top of the Venison Shanks recipe above.

Crockpot Venison Bourguignon

Start the meat marinating in the refrigerator one day in advance of the day you plan to cook the Bourguignon. This is the stand-out recipe for slow cooking venison with mushrooms for a winter stew.

Secret: For this dish, make sure you buy pancetta or the best quality dry cured bacon you can afford. Don't make the mistake of buying "maple" flavored bacon. The maple flavoring, just the same as that used in Aunt Jemima's syrup is actually from fenugreek. Fenugreek belongs in Indian curry powder, but not in Bourguignon! For that matter smoked bacon doesn't either, but this is America!

Marinade Ingredients (place in plastic Ziploc bag in fridge):

2 lbs. venison stew meat in large pieces (1½ to 2" cubes)

1 onion peeled and chopped finely

2 carrots peeled & chopped finely

2 large garlic cloves minced

2 cups red table wine

3 - 4 tbsp. olive oil

1 bay leaf

Handful of chopped fresh parsley

½ tsp. dried thyme leaves

½ tsp. very coarsely ground black pepper

½ tsp. salt (no more, remember the bacon has salt too)

Other Ingredients:

2-3 strips thick-cut bacon cut into 1" pieces

3 tbsp. flour (or rice flour if gluten free)

3 tbsp. olive oil or reserved bacon grease

12 oz small white button mushrooms wiped clean

½ lb. of very small whole pearl onions peeled

3 tbsp. brandy (opt.)

Directions:

One day ahead, place all of the ingredients in the Marinade Ingredients in a gallon size plastic Ziplok bag. Store in refrigerator overnight or up to 24 hours. When ready to cook, remove the meat from the marinade and allow it to drain thoroughly for a few minutes until no more marinade drips from the meat. Catch all of the marinade, and save all of the marinade including the chopped vegetables and spices, etc. We are going to use this marinade later!

Presuming you want to serve this dish for supper, and you are going to start preparing this dish in the morning, set the Crockpot on the counter and turn it on low and plan for it to cook all day. If you start at mid-day, (no later than 3:00 PM), turn the Crockpot on high and plan to let it cook for 2½ hours on high.

In a large heavy bottom skillet or Dutch oven, fry the bacon to lightly brown it. Remove all the bacon and place it in the bottom of the Crockpot. Next brown the venison in batches making sure to sear the pieces on all sides. Don't overcrowd the pan. Remove the browned venison to the Crockpot in batches.

After removing the last of the browned venison, place the pearl onions in the pan & cook on medium high heat for 10 minutes. This will help develop the nice brown color for the broth, and the rich flavor you want. Now transfer all of the pearl onions into the crock pot. Do the same with the mushrooms next.

Next, take the 3 tbsp. of flour, and dust it into the pan, and add the reserved 3 tbsp. of bacon grease or olive oil, stirring to make a roux. Cook on medium high heat until the flour bubbles and begins to toast to a light brown no darker than the color of a brown paper grocery bag.

Carefully quench the hot roux by pouring the entire contents of the marinade bag (wine, chopped vegetables, spices, etc.) and brandy into the cooking pan. Raise the heat and scrape the bottom of the pan to insure that all of the roux is incorporated into the liquid. When the marinade begins to steam and boil, pour it into the crock pot.

Put the lid on the crock pot and cook all day on low, or 2½ - 3 hours on high. Adjust salt at the end of cooking if desired.

Serve with boiled potatoes finished with lots of melted butter.

Brouffade Mariniere
Venison with a Huguenot Flavor

This is a recipe of the French mariners who took barges from the Mediterranean Sea up the Rhone River into the heart of France. It is another great Crockpot recipe. Don't be afraid of the anchovies. Anchovies have great umami, the most recently discovered flavor component. The use of seafood along side of terrestrial meats is quite common in the Mediterranean. Remember, the Romans made a fish sauce called garum, and they transported it all over the known world in amphorae (large bottles). So, this recipe might even have a little Roman influence by using the anchovies to enhance the flavor.

In his 1985 book Southern Cooking, Bill Neal includes a recipe called "Venison Stew". In his words, "A strong French influence marks this cold weather dish of the Huguenot community." He is right. While I don't use the orange peel Bill Neal calls for in his recipe, I do use the anchovies. The orange peel called for in Bill Neal's recipe is however an ingredient in the next recipe Chevreuil en Daube. Both this recipe and the next are inspired by the cooking of the South of France, which coincidentally is where many of the Huguenots (French Protestants) came from. Before and after the Revocation of the Edict of Nantes in 1685, France's loss was Carolina's gain as refugees arrived. Charleston's first 45 Huguenots came in 1680 aboard the sailing ship Richmond.

I frequently prepare a dish to take to the Sunday lunch we have after nearly every Sunday Liturgy and Sermon at the Huguenot Church here in Charleston. Whenever I make one of these venison dishes I can attest there is still a strong affinity for these flavors among Huguenots. Plus ca change, plus ca rest la meme chose. I have caught Tommy Lemacks taking home a little tub of the broth after all of the meat is gone from the pot, and John Hilton is a big lover of venison fixed this way too! These are constant companion recipes for me, and I hope they will become standards for you too.

Lastly, when I attended business school in Chapel Hill in 1983-1985 Bill Neal's restaurant Crooks Corner was a very popular hangout for us. We frequently went there late after studying, and sat around after the dinner crowd left and ordered Spaten beer and barbeque sandwiches. Bill Neal played a huge part in the re-discovery of the Southern kitchen, and I feel very privileged to have been a witness (and patron) to his early success in Chapel Hill, right down to the Buttermilk Sky Pie!

Ingredients:

2 lbs. venison cut into slices

4 - 5 tbsp. olive oil

1 tbsp. red wine or Balsamic vinegar

1 onion chopped fine

½ tsp. dried thyme

3 cloves garlic chopped

2 bay leaves

1 cup red wine (Cotes du Rhone if possible)

2 medium sized sour pickles, diced

2 tbsp. Dijon mustard

3 tbsp. capers, drained

2 oz. can anchovy fillets, drained

Salt & fresh ground black pepper to taste

Directions:

Put meat, the wine, vinegar, garlic, onions, herbs, capers, mustard, 2 tbsp. of the oil, salt & pepper in a shallow covered dish & refrigerate overnight to marinate. Or put in a Ziploc bag and marinate overnight in the fridge. Take the meat out of the marinade and save the marinade.

Heat 3 tbsp. of the oil in a fry pan, and brown the sliced meat using medium high heat. Transfer the browned meat to the Crockpot set on low. Pour the marinade into the fry pan and bring to a simmer. Then pour the hot marinade over the meat in the Crockpot, and add the anchovies. Cook all day set on low while you are at work. When you get home, remove the meat to a serving plate. Then put the crock containing all of the cooking liquid in the oven set on 400 degrees and cook it for about 20 minutes uncovered to reduce the juices and to concentrate them. Finally, add the diced pickles and stir them into the sauce.

Drizzle the meat on the serving plate with olive oil, and pour the rich sauce from the crock pot all around the meat on the serving plate. Serve with mashed potatoes or with pasta.

Chevreuil en Daube
French Slow Roasted Venison

Ingredients:

2 lbs. venison cut into large stew chunks (2")

4 - 5 tbsp. olive oil

1 med. onion chopped

1 med. onion peeled, whole, studded with a 2-3 whole cloves

4 thin strips of fatback or salt pork or

1 nice strip of country ham skin with about ¼" fat left on

2 large tomatoes peeled and chopped

1 bay leaf

Small handful parsley chopped

½ tsp. dried thyme

4 cloves garlic chopped

¼ tsp. quatre epice (white pepper, nutmeg, cloves & ginger)

1 cup red wine

Strip of orange peel with white lining removed

Handful of pitted oil-cured black olives

Salt & fresh ground black pepper to taste

Directions:

Put the meat, wine, garlic, 2 tbsp. of the oil, quatre epice, thyme, bay leaf, and the salt and pepper in a shallow covered dish and refrigerate overnight to marinate. Or put it all in a Ziploc bag and marinate overnight in the fridge. Take the meat out of the marinade and drain it. Don't pour out the marinade. We're using it later! In a fry pan, brown the salt meat or ham skin lightly (not crispy!), and then add the onions to the fat, and cook them until they are translucent. Remove the onions and salt meat to the Crockpot. Heat the rest of the olive oil in the fry pan, and brown the venison. Transfer browned meat to the Crockpot and set it on low. Settle the whole onion with the clove down in the middle of the meat so it is touching the bottom of the crock pot and surrounded by the meat and onions.

Pour the marinade into the fry pan and add the orange peel, the tomatoes and parsley, and bring to a simmer. Then pour the hot marinade over the meat, and cook all day in the Crockpot set on low while you are at work. When you get home, remove the lid & put in the pitted oil-cured olives. Then put the crock in the oven set on 400 degrees and cook it for about 10 -15 min. uncovered to concentrate juices. Serve with bread, millas (re-fried polenta), pasta or rice.

Estofado de Venudo
Venison Stewed in Smoked Spanish Paprika

This dish features the unusual flavor of smoked Spanish paprika (pimenton). It is reminiscent of the flavor of Spanish chorizo which also contains pimenton.

Pimenton, aside from being a coloring and flavoring spice obtained from dried peppers, also has preservative properties. This helps the dried chorizo to cure and avoid spoilage with only the use of salt and no nitrates or nitrites. Sweet Spanish smoked pimenton is widely available at gourmet & health food stores now. Or you can order pimenton on line from La Tienda (www.tienda.com).

Ingredients:

2 lb. venison stew meat in large cubes
1 onion finely chopped
4 cloves garlic
3 tbsp. smoked Spanish paprika (pimenton)
½ cup red table wine
⅓ cup brandy
¼ cup olive oil
Salt & fresh ground pepper
1 bayleaf

Directions:

Put the meat in a covered bowl or Ziploc bag with the wine and brandy. Refrigerate overnight. When ready to cook the dish, drain meat completely, and reserve the marinade. In a large nonstick skillet, pour half the oil, & heat on med-high. Add onions and garlic. Sauté until just browned. Remove the onions and garlic and reserve. Add the rest of the oil, heat to med-high in the same skillet, and then add the meat in two batches, browning all sides quickly to sear the outside. When all of the meat is browned, return the onions, bayleaf, and garlic to the pan with all of the meat. Next, add the smoked paprika (pimenton) by sprinkling it over the meat, and then add the reserved wine & brandy marinade. Season with about ¾ tsp. salt and ½ tsp. fresh ground black pepper or to taste. Cover the pan and lower the heat to simmer. Simmer covered until sauce is thick & meat is very tender. Can be transferred from the skillet to cook in a Crockpot if desired.

Khoresht Baadenjaan
Persian Stewed Venison, Onion & Eggplant

Looking back in time, long before the current concern about Iran's intentions to become a nuclear power, this land used to be known as Persia. Situated in time between the Babylonian captivity of Israel, and the later Greek and Roman Empires, the Persians ruled the known world.

The familiar story of Haman the ruthless prime minister to King Xerxes comprises the entire Biblical book of Esther. To this day, during Purim, the beautiful Jewish girl-queen Esther is credited with having saved Israel from Haman's plan to exterminate the Jews while they were being held in Persian captivity. Regardless, the Persian cuisine is one I am learning more about, and for what I know, it is a delightful, refined, and subtle way of cooking. I particularly like the very subtle and agreeable use of spices. And onions!

My first exposure to anything Iranian was through my classmate Majid Manajemi at NC State in about 1979. Iran was holding American hostages then, and ill feelings between the US and Iran were very high, while they have never been so good since our CIA upset Mosadegh and put Shah Reza Palevi in power in 1953. I had several Iranian friends at NC State, but rumor had it that Majid was related to the Shah, and he was not so popular with the other Middle Eastern students as a result. One night he invited me to his apartment, and I remember he made a Persian dish of chicken, and served it with their characteristic yellow saffron rice (chelou). He had some olives and other garnishes, and I remember it being an altogether very sophisticated meal to come from a college student.

If international diplomacy was centered on food versus ideology, its likely folks would find much more common ground. I have met numerous Iranian people over the years, and in every case have found them very gracious, intelligent, and gentle. I don't like the saber rattling going on in Tehran any more than the next guy, but I sure like this traditional Persian recipe for lamb or beef that suits itself perfectly well for cooking a venison stew.

Venison International

Ingredients:

1 lb. boneless venison cut into 1" cubes
1 large eggplant, or 3-4 long thin Japanese eggplants
3 - 4 tbsp. cooking oil
1 large onion peeled and sliced thinly
3 - 4 tbsp. tomato paste
¾ tsp. ground cinnamon
½ tsp. ground turmeric
¼ tsp. ground nutmeg
¼ tsp. fresh ground black pepper
1 whole lemon or lime
1 tsp. salt
2 cups water

Directions:

If mature and tough, peel the large eggplant. If using a tender eggplant, or the Japanese eggplant, leave the peel on. Cut the large eggplant into quarters, then eights in strips. If using Japanese eggplants, just cut in half lengthwise to make 2 strips. Put the eggplant strips in an earthen baking dish, drizzle with salt and olive oil, and place in the oven on 350 degrees to bake for about 30 min. while you prepare the rest of the dish. When the eggplant is softened and nearly done, remove from the oven and set it aside while the sauce and meat cooks (below).

Heat the oil in a skillet, and sauté the onion until wilted and transparent, then remove the onions to a bowl. Then brown the meat on all sides. Return the cooked onion to the pan. Add the spices, the tomato paste, the juice of the entire lemon or lime, and the 2 cups of water. Bring to a brisk simmer, and cover. Cook covered for about 1¼ hours. Check occasionally to make sure the sauce is not reducing down to the point of scorching. Add more water as needed to prevent burning. The sauce should begin to thicken, and take on a nice rich color. No thickening is to be added to the sauce. Cook until the meat is completely tender. Pour the sauce and meat over the eggplant strips in the earthen dish. Cover the dish, and place in the oven long enough to heat the eggplant and sauce through entirely. Serve with long grain or Basmati rice cooked Persian style (Chelou).

{45}

Chelou
Rice Persian Style

Persian cooking is of particular interest to anyone interested in the rice kitchen. Charleston being the center of the New World rice culture, certainly we owe a nod to the Persian kitchen. Most main dishes in the cuisine are intended to be served with rice. After rice came to Persia 3,000 years ago it became central to the cuisine. From there it spread to Israel where it became popular, and later via the Arab influence, to Spain. As a result, we see evidence of rice as a revered staple in the subsequent cuisines that came in contact with these influences, even here in South Carolina. Our Lowcountry perlow (chicken with rice), or other variations of that word (pilau, pilaf, etc.) all trace to the Persian word polo, meaning rice cooked with meats, vegetables, fruits or herbs.

The point is to end up with beautifully cooked separate grains and with a nice rice crust on the bottom of the pan. This crust is called the "tadiq", and it is the best part. Washing the rice is very important to remove the starch that can make it stick together. Classically, long soaking of the rice is employed, and the rice is then cooked (steamed) in a covered pan with little or no water. Notice any similarity to the old Charleston prescription for cooking rice in a Charleston Rice Steamer?

It is important to use long grain or Basmati rice for this. Not medium or short grain rice which tends to soften and stick together. Long grain rice is high in amylase starch. Shorter grain rice contains less amylase and more amyl pectin, which tends to soften and become gelatinous on cooking (desirable for risotto and paella, but not for rice like this Persian rice or our Lowcountry long grain rice cooked "proper").

Ingredients:

1 cup white long grain or basmati rice

Triple wash rice by rubbing it in a sieve under running water.

2 cups water: first 1 cup, then 2 separate ½ cup stages

¼ tsp. ground turmeric or a few threads of saffron

2 - 3 tbsp. butter or vegetable oil

Pinch salt

Directions:

After washing the rice put it in a heavy bottom sauce pan with a well fitted lid. Ideally use a pot with a glass lid so you can monitor the rice cooking through the lid. Starting with the pan uncovered, add 1 cup water, pinch of salt, and the turmeric (or saffron) to the rice and put it on the stove to heat. Cook on medium high, boiling away most of the water. Add ½ cup water and continue cooking until nearly dry again. This should all take about 5-7 minutes. No more than 8-10 minutes. Finally, add the last ½ cup water, and place the tight lid on the pan. Lower the heat and cook for another 10 min. on low without taking off the lid. Then take off the lid and place a lump of butter or a couple tablespoons full of oil right in the center of the rice. Don't stir. Put the lid back on, and bring the heat back up to medium for another 4-5 minutes, or as long as needed to form a dried, oily rice crust on the bottom of the pan without scorching it. Take the lid off while still steaming hot, and serve. Be sure to scrape some of the bottom crust up when you take a serving.

Hungarian Goulash
with Venison

The first deer I ever killed was a nice doe on a South Carolina gameland near White Oak, SC. I was using a Knight in-line muzzle loader. Nearby I found a bearded hermit who was originally from Maine, and he had a little refrigerated truck body set up behind his cabin, and he butchered deer for people. So I unloaded my deer, and came back a couple of weeks later and retrieved my meat, all wrapped up in butcher's paper. It was like being transported back in time to the early 1900's out there in Fairfield County. One thing I learned from that bearded man was traditional butchery and cuts of meat. Because he was not automated, I got traditional roasts, stew, and steaks. No burger, and no cube steaks.

One of the first things I cooked with that venison was goulash. The L. L. Bean Cookbook has a nice recipe called "Venison Stew Paprika". It is masquerading, but it is goulash.

Goulash is Eastern European, and variations of it occur in Europe's forested regions where people have been feeding on deer since they were drawing pictures on the inside of caves in Europe. Goulash comes from the word gulyas, the Hungarian for cattleman or herdsman. There are however variations on goulash using venison too, so we are right in line with tradition.

The defining thing about goulash is the use of paprika. No paprika, no goulash! While Spanish paprika is fine, since goulash is Eastern European, plan to buy a can of Szeged Hungarian paprika, and after opening it, keep it in the refrigerator to insure it stays fresh. Although hot paprika is available, the sweet paprika is the most versatile and it is what we need here.

Ingredients:

1½ lb. venison stew meat cut in small cubes (1")

2 - 3 oz. smoked thick cut bacon

Flour

2 med. onions sliced thinly

3 cloves garlic

1 bell pepper (preferably red and ripe, green ok)

2 carrots, peeled and diced very finely

2 tbsp. tomato paste

¼ cup paprika

1 tsp. dried marjoram

1 lg. bay leaf

1 cup prepared beef or chicken stock

½ cup white wine or beer

½ tsp. caraway seeds (opt.)

1 cup sauerkraut (opt.)

Directions:

Sautee the bacon in a large non-stick skillet, fry pan, or Dutch oven. Remove the bacon from the grease when fully rendered. Keep the bacon to add back to the pot.

Season the meat with salt and pepper, and dredge in flour, shaking off the excess. Brown the meat in the bacon grease making sure there is room in the pan for the meat to brown and sear on the outside. Remove the meat to a plate.

Add the onions to the fry pan, and cook until they soft and beginning to caramelize. Add the garlic, peppers, and carrots and sauté until all of the vegetables are wilted. Next add the seasonings including the paprika, marjoram, bay leaf, and the tomato paste. Stir to mix well.

Next add the broth, & wine (or beer), and bring to a boil. Return the browned meat and bacon to the pan. If you are using the sauerkraut and caraway seeds, add them at this point also.

At this point you can transfer the goulash to a Crockpot to finish cooking slowly all day or overnight on the low setting, or you can simmer it on the stove top covered. Monitor it to make sure it does not stick or dry out if you cook it on the stove at least 1½ hours. The goulash should thicken up nicely as it cooks and reduces. Long slow cooking is the key, and you can use your lesser cuts of venison for this as long as you are willing to wait it out while the heavenly smell fills your kitchen.

Serve the goulash with a dollop of sour cream on top of each individual serving if you like.

Serve with egg noodles, steamed rice, or buttered boiled potatoes.

Corned Venison Boiled Dinner

The word "corned" does not refer to corn on the cob. Corned means salted, as the Old English "corns" or grains of salt. Either rubbed with salt or brined is the way to obtain corned meat. Growing up in Fayetteville, NC we would occasionally go to eat on holidays with our great friend Rachel Wilson, a great Southern cook who grew up in Clio, SC. I distinctly remember her serving "corned ham". This was a fresh ham, brine cured, but not dried out like a country ham. It was not smoked, but it was delicious! So there is corned beef, corned ham, and of course corned venison.

My wife went to school at Simmons College in Boston. It was an all women's college. Whenever I cook a boiled dinner she clears out, and complains about the smell. She kvetches about them serving New England Boiled Dinner at Simmons. She always boycotted that meal! Regardless, my last name is Mullin, and that being an Irish name, I like my boiled dinner. Enjoy!

Corned Venison Ingredients:

Venison shoulder roast or flank rolled & tied with, cotton twine

1 tbsp. Morton "Tender Quick" cure per pound of meat

1 - 2 tbsp. brown sugar

1 tbsp. fresh ground black pepper

1 tbsp. sweet paprika

1 tsp. garlic powder

1 tsp. ground allspice

Ingredients for the Boil:

Corned venison roast

1 cabbage washed and quartered

½ lb. carrots peeled & chunked

2 - 3 turnips peeled and quartered

1 small rutabaga peeled & halved

3 - 4 medium size peeled whole onions

5 - 6 stalks celery washed and cut in half

1½ lb. waxy boiling potatoes skins on (Red Bliss, Yukon)

3 - 4 whole cloves garlic

2 bay leaves

¼ cup olive oil

Meat Cure Directions:

Mix all of the spice and cure ingredients together, and rub evenly on the roast. If using a flank, lay it out flat, and coat all sides with the dry rub. Then roll the flank up tightly and secure with several pieces of cotton kitchen twine. Note: Morton's Tender Quick is available on line at mortonsalt.com (Click on Meat Curing and go to the online store). Also online at Heinsohn's Country Store at texastastes.com. Place meat in a plastic Ziploc bag and put in the bottom of the refrigerator. Turn a couple of times per day. Leave to cure for 7 days in the refrigerator.

Cooking the Dinner:

Remove the corned roast from the Ziploc bag, and briefly rinse it under running water. In a large heavy bottomed pot, place the roast with the garlic, and bay leaf, (and rutabaga if using one). Just cover it with cold water. Bring to a rapid boil over high heat, and skim off any scum and foam that forms at the beginning. Reduce the heat and simmer for about 2 hours until the meat is tender and shrunken. It should remain pink like a corned beef brisket.

Remove the lid, and place the vegetables around and on top of the meat. Put the top back on, and raise the heat again to a boil, and steam the vegetables for about 30-40 minutes. Turn off the heat, and allow to sit for 15 minutes covered.

When ready to serve, remove the roast and vegetables to a large serving bowl on the table, and ladle broth around it to keep everything warm. Strain and serve some broth in individual bowls as a first course if desired.

Suggested Accompaniments:

Pickled okra

Prepared Dijon mustard

Green tomato mostarda

Russian Sweet & Sour Venison

Ingredients:

2 - 3 lbs. boneless venison roast

2 - 3 tbsp. cooking oil

1 lg. onion peeled and chopped medium

1 carrot peeled and chopped

1 bay leaf

2 - 3 tbsp. butter

1½ tbsp. brown sugar

¼ cup red wine vinegar

2 tbsp. tomato paste

½ tsp. ground allspice

¼ cup raisins

½ lb. whole small tender beets peeled or larger beets chopped

½ tsp. very coarsely ground black pepper

1 tsp. salt

Directions:

Cut the roast into thick slices about 1½" to 2" thick. Salt and pepper the roast slices, and brown on both sides on medium low in the oil in a deep Dutch oven or skillet for about 10 - 15 minutes. Remove the meat from the pan and hold on a plate or if using a Crockpot, place the browned meat slices in the Crockpot.

Add onions and carrots to the pan, along with the butter, and sauté the onion and carrots for about 10 minutes until the vegetables are wilted. Add the red wine vinegar, beets, bay leaf, tomato paste, raisins, allspice, and sugar, and heat to a simmer.

Add the meat back to the pan, and cover. Place in the oven to bake for about 1½ to 2 hours on 300 degrees, or until tender.

If using the Crockpot, place the roast slices in the crock pot, and pour the hot vegetables and sauce around the roast, and put the lid on. Cook all day on low, or cook for about 2 to 2½ hours in the Crockpot on high.

Fast Cooked Venison

If I Killed a Deer

Lowcountry Mustard Fried Venison

When I worked as a well logging engineer in the offshore Louisiana Oilfield a frequent oil rig entrée was "chicken fried steak". This is just chicken fried venison cube steak with a flavorful twist.

1½ lbs. venison cube steaks
Yellow mustard
Salt
Fresh ground black pepper
Flour
Cooking oil

Directions:

Several hours before mealtime, smear both sides of the cube steaks with a copious amount of mustard, and salt and pepper to taste. Cover, and return to the fridge to marinate. Just before you want to eat, take the steaks out of the fridge, drain any excess liquid, dredge in flour, and shake off the excess flour. Stack the steaks on a plate. Heat about ¾" of cooking oil in a black iron skillet or use a deep fat fryer. Drop several steaks into the oil, but don't crowd them. They need to cook quickly so they sear on the outside and stay moist and flavorful on the inside. As soon as the outside breading is golden brown, remove and drain on a paper towel and serve immediately.

Variations:

1) Mix an equal amount of Pepsi with the mustard, cover the steaks with this marinade mix, and marinate the steaks overnight. Dredge in flour and fry as above.

2) Mix a couple tablespoons of Worcestershire Sauce with the mustard, cover the steaks with this marinade mix, and marinate the steaks overnight. Dredge in flour and fry as above.

3) Mix a couple of tablespoons of soy sauce with the mustard, cover the steaks with this marinade mix, and marinate the steaks overnight. Eliminate salt. Dredge in flour and fry as above.

4) On any of the above recipes, you can break an egg, add 1 tbsp. water, scramble it, and dip the steaks in this egg wash before dredging them in the flour. This makes for a more thick crust tempura style.

Brandied Venison Loin Steaks
with Clemson Blue Cheese Butter

In spite of the fact I am a graduate of the other Carolina cow college, NC State, the first time I tasted the blue cheese they make up at Clemson University I was hooked. Ever since I was a kid, I have loved the flavor of blue cheese anyway. Straight from the Clemson website:

"CLEMSON – Clemson Blue Cheese was rated among the best in the nation at the 15th biennial United States Championship Cheese Contest in Green Bay, Wis. The United States Championship Cheese Contest is the longest-running cheese competition in the nation. The artisan cheese is made traditionally, using 288-gallon vats. The cheese is then salted and waxed before aging six months.

Clemson Blue Cheese has a history that dates back to 1941, when blue cheese was cured in the damp air of the Stumphouse Mountain Tunnel near Walhalla by a Clemson dairy professor. Now the cheese is made in Clemson's Newman Hall, where air-conditioned rooms replicate the temperatures and humidity of the tunnel.

Clemson Blue Cheese is available for purchase in the East Side Food Court located in the Hendrix Student Center on the Clemson campus or online at www.clemsonbluecheese.com."

Ingredients:

12 - 16 oz. of venison loin steaks cut 1" to 1½" thick

4 - 5 tbsp. brandy (Jacques Cardin is what I use)

1 garlic clove

½ stick butter and,

An equal amount Clemson (or other blue cheese) - 4 oz.

2 tbsp. butter for frying

Salt

Fresh ground black pepper

Directions:

Put the ½ stick of butter and blue cheese out on the counter and allow to come to room temperature. In a small bowl, mash these together thoroughly combining them with a fork or spoon. Scrape the blue cheese compound butter up with a rubber spatula, and lay the mound of it on a piece of plastic wrap. Form it into a log about 1" in diameter, and wrap with the plastic. Place in the refrigerator to firm up for later use.

Place the steaks in single layer in a shallow dish just large enough to hold them.

Pepper them to taste. Don't salt them.

Lay the garlic on the cutting board, and lay the flat blade of a large cooking knife on it. Strike the flat blade with the heel of your hand. Peel garlic, and then mash thoroughly with the knife. Mince completely, and scrape up the mashed garlic, and put it on the steaks.

Next dribble the brandy over the steaks, cover, and then place in the fridge for 3 - 4 hours.

Remove the steaks from the fridge about 30-45 minutes before you plan to cook them and let them warm up to near room temperature on the counter. When ready to cook, remove the steaks from the marinade, drain them, and reserve the marinade.

Cooking:

Heat a couple of tablespoons of butter in a non-stick skillet on medium high. Making sure the steaks are not crowded in the skillet, sear the steaks quickly on each side in the butter, turning only once (about 2-3 minutes per side depending on your preference whether red, pink, or God-forbid well done (don't even consider it!).

Remove the steaks to a plate warmed in the oven. Deglaze the skillet with the reserved marinade to make a simple sauce. Add a little salt at this point if desired.

Pour the pan juice over the steaks, then top each one with a slice of the blue-cheese compound butter from your little log. Serve immediately.

Heribert von Feilizsch's
Whole Roast Venison Loin

As this cookbook was coming together I contacted a friend on his farm in Northern Virginia to see if he would give me a venison recipe. While building the Cassique Garden Cottages for Kiawah Development, I met Harry through his company Henselstone Window and Door. Henselstone imports and installs a beautiful line of German made tilt-turn windows that we used exclusively in building this group of homes. Having spent some time together, I knew Harry was a hunter, and in fact he butchers his own game. He is meticulous in everything he does, so this recipe comes on good authority from a man who is a hunter, a cook, and a lover of good food and wine. He's pretty good company to be around at the table too! I can't add a thing to Harry's contribution, so the unabridged email from Harry follows here in the directions.

Remember I told you to take control over the cuts of venison you get back from your butcher. This recipe will require you to make sure they get you the whole loin, ribs as specified, with tenderloins and back straps intact on both sides of the spine. I told Harry this was a caveman size roast. His answer, "If you shot a caveman size deer. You could on a larger deer cut it into roasts between the vertebrae". Isn't that what every hunter wants? To shoot a caveman size deer!

Several weeks later my wife Janice and I took a trip to New York's Upper West side. I picked up a book I spied on the table of a used bookseller on Broadway about a block from Zabars. It was a Time-Life book published in 1969, and it was titled The Cooking of Germany. Miraculously, when I opened the book to examine it, to my amazement there was a full page color photo of the same roast Harry described above. And the following page contained the recipe along with two diagrams showing how to lard the roast and carve it.

Ingredients:

1 venison roast described in Directions below

1 bottle red table wine

Fresh rosemary

2 - 3 lbs. potatoes

1 apple

Salt & fresh ground black pepper

Butter and flour

Beef stock

Directions:

"In Germany we cut the deer up a little different. We cut the ribs about 3" below the spine and leave the inner and outer tenderloin attached to the bone. After the deer is hung two or three weeks, I spike the tenderloins with inch-long fat cubes every three inches or so. Then I add salt, pepper, fresh rosemary and pour half a bottle of red wine over it, collecting in the pan. I also put half an apple in the pan. The rack gets baked for 15 to 20 minutes at 500 degrees. It should still have a bloody center. When cutting the meat off the bone it will finish out on its own to be medium. I make the sauce with the drippings from the rack, some more red wine and beef stock. It is thickened with a little bit of flour. I serve the meal with quartered potatoes, boiled to almost done and then broiled in butter until slightly brown. When I serve them I add some Italian parsley. As a green vegetable I use either green beans or asparagus." Heribert von Feilizsch

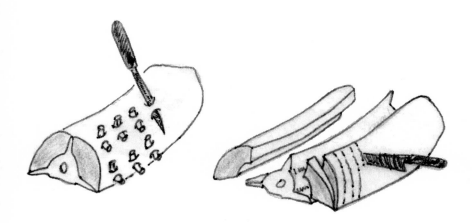

Fegato di Cervo alla Venezia
Venison Liver with Sautéed Onions

Sometimes I will shoot a couple of yearling does just for meat. In fact I did that on one of the last days of the season in 2008, and drove my two little deer down to Cordray's, which took nearly 2 hours from my place up in Williamsburg County! Thankfully it was cold.

I asked Michael Cordray to save me the livers and hearts, and clearly not many folks do that. He said they have been trying to get the State of South Carolina DHEC to let them process organ meats into pet food. That was one of the best ideas I had heard in a long time. Where else but the USA would we throw away all of that wholesome meat? Of course we need laws on the books preventing the sale of game meat, but this is a byproduct that surely could be adequately regulated while still preventing such a waste.

The key is to never overcook the liver. It should be seared on each side quick and hot to seal it. Serve immediately from the pan just like you would rush a rare steak on a warmed plate to the table.

Ingredients:
12 - 16 oz. of venison liver. Trimmed, and sliced ¼" thick
1 large onion thinly sliced
3 - 4 tbsp. butter
2 tbsp. olive oil
Salt
Fresh ground black pepper
½ lemon
Handful fresh parsley-chopped

Options:
Dredge liver slices in flour and shake off excess & brown.
Or, substitute 2 tbsp. Balsamic vinegar juice of ½ lemon above.

Directions:

Melt half of the butter and half of the olive oil in a non-stick skillet. Cook the onions in the oil for about 20 minutes until they completely wilt, and begin to caramelize. Scrape the onions from the pan to a warm plate and put in the oven set on warm.

Add the rest of the butter and oil to the pan, and heat on med-high. Salt and pepper the liver, and as soon as the butter bubbles and then the bubbles subside, put the thin strips of liver in the pan, allowing plenty of space between them for them to sear evenly without touching each other.

After about 1 minute on the first side, flip them to the other side. Cook that side for a minute, then remove from the pan and put on the plate on top of the pile of onions. Quickly de-glaze the pan with the juice of the half lemon (or use a couple of tablespoons of Balsamic Vinegar if desired instead). Pour the pan juices over the cooked liver and onions, sprinkle with the parsley, and take to the table.

Bacon Wrapped Tournedos
with Dry Mustard Butter

Ingredients:

12 - 16 oz. of venison tenderloin steaks cut 1½" thick

Thick cut smoked bacon

½ stick butter

2 tbsp. dry mustard powder

Juice of ¼ lemon

2 tbsp. minced fresh chives

¼ tsp. fresh ground black pepper

Directions:

Put the butter out on the counter and allow to come to room temperature. In a small bowl, mash the butter and the dry mustard powder until well blended combining them with a fork or spoon. Add minced chives, fresh ground pepper, salt (omit if using salted butter), and lemon juice, and mix again. Scrape the compound butter up with a rubber spatula, and lay the mound of it on a piece of plastic wrap. Form it into a log about 1" in diameter, and wrap with the plastic. Place in the refrigerator to firm up for later use.

Next, wrap each tenderloin steak tightly with a strip of bacon, and use several toothpicks, or a short piece of kitchen twine tied around to secure the end of the bacon. Heat an iron frying pan that will just hold all of your steaks, and lay an extra 2 - 3 pieces of bacon on it to render out the fat. Remove the bacon. Having about ¼" or more of bacon grease is desirable so it comes up on the side of the steaks about ½ inch when you have them all in the pan. Then salt and pepper each steak, and place the individual steaks on the fry pan with space in between. Fry the steaks quickly to the desired doneness. About 3 minutes per side.

Remove the steaks from the pan, place them on a warmed plate, and top each one with a pat of the dry mustard compound butter sliced from the butter log. Crumble the cooked bacon over the steaks. Serve immediately while piping hot.

Pan Seared Venison
with Bobby Flay's Espresso Dry Rub

The Sept. 8, 2007 Weekend Journal section of The Wall Street Journal had an article called "The Search for the Perfect Steak" by Katy McLaughlin. The combination of cooking in a heavy cast iron skillet and the spice rub is good with venison too!

Ingredients:

Venison steaks cut 2" thick

Bobby Flay's Steak Rub (below)

Grape seed or canola oil

Bobby Flay's Espresso Dry Rub for Beefsteak (or Venison!)

¼ cup ancho chili powder

¼ cup fine ground espresso coffee

2 tbsp. sweet paprika

2 tbsp. brown sugar

1 tbsp. dry mustard

1 tbsp. salt

1 tbsp. fresh ground black pepper

1 tbsp. dried oregano

1 tbsp. ground coriander

2 tsp. ground ginger

2 tsp. chili de arbol powder or cayenne (optional)

Keep in the fridge in a small Mason jar

Directions:

Take steaks out of the fridge 1 hour before cooking (less if in hot weather). Dry the meat with a paper towel. Preheat oven to 400 degrees. Heat a heavy cast iron skillet outdoors (or indoors if you have good kitchen ventilation). Shake a wet hand over it. Heat until the little drops form balls of water that dance across the iron & turn to steam. Season steaks on both sides with the rub. Brush oil on the bottom of the pan. Put the steaks in the iron pan with some space between and sear for 2 minutes on the first side. Flip and sear the second side for 2 minutes, turning once. Remove the pan from the flame and place in oven for 5 minutes. Set pan on the table on an insulated trivet with foil over the steaks to rest 5 min. Deglaze the pan with a little water after serving the meat and spoon a little pan juice over each steak.

If I Killed a Deer

Ground Venison

Hachis Parmentier
Ground Venison & Mashed Potato Pie

At one time the potato was so closely associated with Antoine-Augustin Parmentier that it was called "une parmentier". This dish is similar to shepherd's pie, or even a "twice baked" potato. The variations are endless. Traditionally the meat would have been the shredded, chopped left over meat from a boiled dinner or roast. Using ground meat makes it easier to prepare with what you have on hand. This is a very kid-friendly dish too. Serve with a salad for a simple meal.

Ingredients:

1 pound ground venison

1 clove garlic mashed & minced

1 Tbsp. flour (or rice flour)

½ tsp. dried thyme leaves

1½ pounds white potatoes

1 cup grated cheese (Gruyere, Parmigiano, etc.)

1 tender rib celery chopped finely (optional)

Salt & fresh ground pepper to taste

1 large onion peeled & diced

2 - 3 tbsp. butter

1 large ripe tomato-peeled & diced

1 - 2 raw egg yolks

Directions:

Wash the potatoes & boil in salted water. Drain, & allow to cool. When cool, remove skins & mash potatoes well with a fork, or with a ricer or food processor. The hashis may be made with whipped potatoes, or very coarsely mashed potatoes with chunks, depending on preference. Add half the grated cheese to the potatoes & mix. Set aside for now.

Heat the butter & sauté onion and garlic (and celery if using it) until the onions are transparent. Add tomatoes and cook for 5 minutes. Remove from the heat, & transfer the cooked vegetables to a bowl. Stir in the tablespoonful of flour and mix well with the vegetables. Next brown the venison in a little more butter. Season with salt, pepper & the thyme. When meat is nicely browned, add back the vegetables, and stir all ingredients together. Set aside to cool for about 15 minutes. When cooled, add the egg yolk(s), and stir to mix well.

Oil a large shallow Pyrex or ceramic baking dish with a large pat of butter. Then place the meat mixture in the baking dish & spread in a uniform layer on the bottom of the dish. Next turn the mashed potatoes out on top of the meat layer, spreading the potatoes out forming a uniform topping over the meat. Sprinkle the top with the rest of the grated cheese, a few pats of butter, and bake on 400 degrees for about 15-20 minutes until the top is browned, and all ingredients are heated through. Let rest for 5-10 minutes before slicing to serve.

Hamburguesas a la plancha
with Caramelized Onions

Ingredients:

1½ pound ground venison

Cheese (Gruyere, Manchego, Swiss, etc.)

Caramelized onions kept warm (see Sofregit recipe Pg. 118)

Salt

Fresh ground black pepper

Olive oil

Directions:

Take the ground meat out of the refrigerator 20 - 30 minutes before cooking. Leave it on the counter to come up near room temperature. Use a ¼ c. measuring cup to measure the same amount of meat out for each hamburguesa. Make them into patties about ½ inch thick. Dust each side of the burgers with black pepper to taste. Brush each side with a little olive oil.

Heat a well seasoned iron skillet outdoors on a gas flame. Sprinkle the iron with salt. When it is hot, lay the burgers out on the hot iron with space between, and sear the 1st side for about 2 - 3 minutes. Flip the burgers and lay a small thin slice of cheese on each one. Cook for 2 - 3 more minutes on the second side, and remove the burgers and place on individual small buns warmed in the oven. The potato rolls at most grocery stores are just the right size. Put a tablespoonful of warm caramelized onions (see "Sofregit" Pg. 118) on top of the cheese on each hamburguesa & finish with a decorative toothpick that has the frilly plastic on top. Stack on a platter and take to the table. Make a bunch of these because you will be surprised how they disappear. Serve as an appetizer or as a main dish with iced sangria or cold beer.

Venison Blender Chili
with Home Made Ancho Chili Powder

I have often wondered what goes into chili powder. Most prepared versions have a combination of "chili", oregano, cumin, garlic powder, and salt. Some have silicon dioxide to prevent the spices from sticking together. The "chili" can be of various varieties. Here is a recipe for a home-made chili seasoning using ancho chili, which is a very dark, almost black colored dried pepper that is widely available in the whole dried pepper form. I like to use marjoram instead of oregano. They are both similar in flavor, being in the mint family, but marjoram is softer, and not quite as aggressive. It lets the earthy chili pepper shine through.

Starting with ¼ tsp. you can adjust the heat in your home-made chili powder by the addition of cayenne pepper because ancho peppers are very low on the Scoville heat scale for pepper heat. Ancho peppers have only about 2,000 Scoville Heat Units. Compare that to 30,000 - 50,000 for cayenne peppers. Then compare that to Scotch Bonnet or Habanero peppers which have anywhere from 100,000 - 350,000.

Aside from making your own chili seasoning, the thing that's different about this recipe is the technique. Using a blender to puree all of the vegetables puts the entire focus of the chili on the meat in a delicious flavorful sauce. There are no identifiable pieces of onion, tomatoes, or peppers, but they are all there in the background contributing complexity. I got this idea of making a vegetable puree, and adding the puree to hot oil from Safiatu Braima, my friend and great cook from Sierra Leone. She uses the method in her chicken stewed in peanut butter, a classic West African one-pot meal. Try it on a pot of chili!

Ingredients:

1½ lbs. venison burger

1 can chopped tomatoes (15 oz. can) including all of the juice

1 med. onion chopped

½ sweet bell pepper (green or red)

2 - 3 cloves garlic peeled

3 tbsp. olive oil

1 tsp. salt (omit if using commercial chili powder)

3 tbsp. masa or corn flour

3 cups water (or 1½ cup water plus 1 can of beer)

1 recipe of "Home Made Ancho Chili Powder"

or 3 - 4 tbsp. commercial chili powder (omit the 1 tsp. salt above)

Home Made Ancho Chili Powder - Mix together:

1 large dried ancho chili pepper-grind fine in coffee grinder,
   (About 2½ to 3 tbsp.)

¼ tsp. cayenne pepper

1 tsp. dried marjoram

1 tsp. sweet paprika

1 tsp. ground cumin

½ tsp. garlic powder

Directions:

In a blender, combine the onion, can of tomatoes, half bell pepper and garlic cloves, and blend until the contents are reduced to a fine puree. Set aside.

Heat a heavy bottomed pot and brown the ground meat in two batches on medium high heat. Remove the browned meat to a bowl and reserve until later If using fatty ground meat, drain off and discard as much of the meat fat as you desire to remove at this point.

Add the olive oil to the pot, and heat over medium high heat to just about the smoking point. Quickly pour the blender full of vegetable puree into the oil to quench the oil's heat, and cook the mixture hot and fast for about 5-10 minutes of hard boiling the puree of vegetables.

Next, add the browned meat back to the pot along with the salt and chili powder seasoning mix (if desired, you can first toast the chili seasoning mix in a small dry skillet before adding it to the pot). Take 1 cup of the water (or beer) in a cup or bowl, and add the masa or corn flour into the water and stir it well to prevent clumping. Add this mix of water and corn flour mix to the chili in the pot, and stir thoroughly. Add the remaining 2 cups of water or beer. Bring the chili to a boil on medium heat, then turn down to simmer for 1 hour with a lid on the pot.

Venison Stuffed Cabbage Rolls

This recipe (which I have modified a little) is one my Grandmother Mary Baber Ellett contributed to a cookbook called Coastal Carolina Cooking. It was put out by the Women's Auxiliary to the Ocean View Memorial Hospital in Myrtle Beach. The hospital is gone, torn down to make room for a condo project that has never been built. And the ladies of the Auxiliary are all gone I am sure since the book was first published in 1958. The foreword is by none other than Dr. Archibald Rutledge, poet laureate of SC. He says, "A hospital is where the Good Samaritan lives".

Even though the recipe appeared in a "Coastal Carolina" cookbook, it is anything but local. My grandparents moved to Myrtle Beach from Pocahontas, Virginia. Pocahontas is famous for its 13 foot tall seam of bituminous coal, and it was a boomtown in the early 1900's. The little town attracted miners of all stripes from all over the world, many Italians, Hungarians, and Slavs among them. The ladies in Pocahontas cooked cabbage rolls for fundraisers, and my grandmother learned this recipe from them. It is clearly of Eastern European origin.

Stuffed cabbage rolls are especially common in the world of Jewish cooking, and they go by many names including dolmas de kol in the Balkans, holishkes or golabki in Poland, gefullte kraut in Germany & Austria, and cavoli ripieni in Italy. This dish got around, and every ethnic group had a different way of spicing it, so feel free to experiment.

Make a big batch, and put some of these cabbage rolls in Ziploc bags in the freezer. When you have a hard day and don't feel like cooking, pull a bag out and heat them up. They are excellent with a salad, and a nice glass of red wine. Coal miners' comfort food!

Ingredients:

1 large head cabbage	1 lb. ground pork or veal
1 lb. ground venison	2 large eggs
½ cup dry white rice	1 large onion
2 - 3 cloves garlic mashed and minced	1½ tsp salt
1 tsp. Worcestershire Sauce	½ tsp. ground marjoram
1 tbsp. sweet paprika	½ tsp. fresh ground black pepper
2 ribs celery	1 red bell pepper
2 bay leaves	¼ cup olive oil
1 lemon	Large can of tomato juice or V-8
Can crushed tomatoes	

Blanching the Cabbage and Separating the Leaves:

Take a paring knife and cut out the stem in a cone shape about 2" deep. In a large pot put 1" water w. the cabbage stem side down. Blanch for about 30 minutes on medium heat to keep it steaming constantly. Remove cabbage from pot and allow to drain and cool. When cool peel leaves off carefully. Make a stack of separate whole leaves. Cut the small core in chunks to add to the pot.

Meat Filling:

Mince the onion finely. In a large mixing bowl break the eggs and scramble well. Add the ground meat, finely minced onion, garlic, salt, black pepper, dry rice, Worcestershire Sauce, and 3-4 tbsp. of the tomato juice. Mix the meat filling with a large spoon or the best way is with your hands. It should be soft and hold together.

Stuffing the Cabbage Leaves:

Put a tablespoon full of meat mixture in each cabbage leaf, using more for the large leaves, and less for the small ones. With the thin leaf edge toward you, fold the right & left edges toward the middle over the meat. Then roll into a neat package finishing with the cabbage leaf's stem showing on the outside of the roll. Use exactly 2 toothpicks on each roll to hold together. Pull 2 toothpicks from each when served.

Cooking the Rolls:

Layer rolls in the bottom of a heavy non-reactive pot. Pour all of the tomato juice in to cover them. Also add a can or two of tomato sauce or canned crushed tomatoes to thicken the sauce a bit. Add the celery, pepper strips, paprika, bay leaves, juice of the lemon, marjoram, and olive oil. Bring the pot to a slow boil then lower heat to a simmer for about 1 hour covered. Cut off the heat and let rest 15-20 min., then serve. Better yet, leave the pot to cool. When cool refrigerate the cabbage rolls and re-heat the next day. They're better the second day!

Pastitsio
Greek Baked Pasta & Ground Venison Pie

Pastitsio is like a baked lasagna, but instead of flat noodles, it uses macaroni, ziti, or any hollow tubular pasta. In Greece, traditionally lamb is the meat, but venison is superb in it. It is easy to understand pastitsio if you realize it involves four steps. Pastitsio can be prepared ahead of a party, and popped in the oven to re-heat. Serve with a Greek salad. See www.kopiaste.org for more Greek recipes. Whether pastitsio is Italian or Greek is a source of speculation and argument. The name comes from the Italian pasticcio al forno, which means oven baked pasta. Maybe the original idea was Italian after all. This recipe is my wife Janice's. Get your dishwasher cleared before starting because this one takes a lot of bowls and different steps. But it is so good it is worth the effort!

Ingredients:
1 lb. dried macaroni, ziti, penne, or other tubular pasta

Meat Sauce:
1½ lbs. ground venison
4 - 5 tbsp. olive oil
1 med. onion chopped fine
1- 15 oz. can crushed tomatoes
¼ cup dry sherry
2 lg. cloves garlic peeled & finely chopped
½ tsp. ground cinnamon
¼ tsp. ground allspice
½ tsp. black pepper
½ tsp. oregano
1 tsp. salt
2 egg yolks

Mornay Sauce-Bechamel Sauce with cheese:
¼ cup butter
4 cups milk
Salt & fresh ground black pepper to taste
1 cup grated Parmigiano cheese

¼ cup flour
2 eggs
¼ tsp. nutmeg

Pasta:

Boil pasta in salted water until not quite done al-dente. Don't overcook until mushy! Remember, the dish will be baked after it is assembled so the pasta cooks more then. Drain & add a couple tbsp. olive oil & toss to coat so it won't stick together as it cools. Set aside.

Meat Sauce:

In a large non-stick skillet, brown the ground meat in half of the olive oil. When done drain grease & stir in cinnamon, allspice, black pepper. Remove meat from skillet, and pour in the sherry to deglaze the pan. Pour the pan juices in the reserved bowl of browned meat and set aside. Wipe out skillet & add remaining olive oil, onions, & garlic. Sautee until translucent. Add back the cooked meat, tomatoes, oregano, & salt. Simmer sauce covered for 30 min. then uncover, and let cool for 15 min. When cool add the 2 egg yolks and blend. This is to help the sauce set up so the pastitsio will cut out in nice squares.

Mornay Sauce (Bechamel Sauce with cheese):

Melt the butter in a clean non-stick skillet, and add flour, cooking few minutes until it begins to have a toasty aroma. Beat the 2 eggs thoroughly & set aside. Add milk gradually in small amounts to the simmering butter & flour, and continue to cook on medium low, whisking constantly. When the sauce has thickened, blend in the grated Parmigiano, salt, pepper to taste, & nutmeg. Stir to blend. Take off the burner and let cool for 10 - 15 minutes. Remove about ½ cup of the warm thickened sauce, & blend in a separate bowl with the beaten eggs to temper them, then gradually dribble that mix of the tempered eggs back into the bulk of the sauce whisking constantly. Don't re-heat the sauce at this point. It will cook again upon baking.

Assembly & Baking:

Generously oil a large rectangular Pyrex baking pan with olive oil or butter. First make a layer with half the cooked pasta. Pour half the meat sauce over it, then a layer of the remaining pasta, then the remaining meat sauce. Flatten the surface down evenly in the rectangular pan. Next, pour the Mornay sauce over the entire top and smooth out evenly so the entire top is covered. Sprinkle generously with Parmigiano cheese, a little dusting of cinnamon, and place on the middle rack in a pre-heated oven set to 350 degrees to bake for about 40 minutes until bubbly & browned on top. Remove and allow to cool for 15 minutes before cutting out in squares.

S.C. Masterpiece BBQ'd Venison Meatloaf

Here's a good use for venison burger.

Ingredients:

1½ lbs. venison burger

2 large eggs

⅔ cup cooked white rice

½ cup Cola BBQ sauce (Recipe Pg. 22 or store-bought sauce)

1 finely minced medium onion

¾ tsp. salt

½ tsp. fresh ground black pepper

½ tsp. garlic powder

Pam cooking spray

2 tbsp. BBQ dry rub (See Cola Ribs recipe) or paprika

2 strips bacon

Directions:

Shell the two eggs in a large mixing bowl, and scramble completely. Add the ground venison, white rice, BBQ sauce, minced onion, salt, black pepper and garlic powder. Mix these ingredients thoroughly with a spoon or with your hands.

Spray the inside of a Pyrex bread pan with cooking spray, then dust the inside of the pan with the dry rub or paprika so you coat the inside of the oiled pan with a thin layer of dry rub or paprika. This will give us a nice flavorful layer on the outside of the meatloaf. It's our "smoke ring".

Pack the ground meat mixture down in the Pyrex pan, and level the surface with a spatula. Sprinkle the top with more dry rub or paprika, and lay the two slices of bacon on the top of the meatloaf lengthwise.

Bake in a hot oven (400 degrees) for about 30 - 35 minutes. Remove from the oven and allow to cool for about 10 - 15 min. to let the meatloaf solidify a little before attempting to cut slices. Serve with a little warmed BBQ sauce on top. Make a side of Tangy Potato Salad Spiked with Okra Pickle Juice.

Parmigiano Portabella Venison Meatloaf

Another nice venison meatloaf.

Ingredients:

1½ lbs. venison burger

2 large eggs

2 - 3 slices bread crumbled

½ lb. baby portabella mushrooms diced fine, sautéed in 2 tbsp. oil

1 finely minced medium onion

¼ cup tomato paste

⅔ cup grated Parmigiano cheese

1 tbsp. balsamic vinegar

1 tsp. salt

½ tsp. fresh ground black pepper

½ tsp. garlic powder

½ tsp. dried thyme leaves

3 bay leaves

2 strips bacon

Directions:

First sauté the diced mushrooms until all of the liquid is released and evaporated & mushrooms begin to brown. Putting raw mushrooms into the meatloaf will release too much liquid into the meatloaf. Cooking the mushrooms first also accentuates their flavor. Shell 2 eggs in a large mixing bowl, & scramble. Add the ground venison, cooked mushrooms, torn bread, cheese, tomato paste, vinegar, minced onion, thyme, salt, black pepper and garlic powder. Mix all ingredients thoroughly with a spoon or with your hands.

Oil the inside of a Pyrex bread pan, and pack the ground meat mixture down into the bread pan. Level the surface of the meat with a spatula. Lay the three bay leaves crosswise on the top of the loaf, and then the two slices of bacon on the top of the meatloaf lengthwise. Bake in a hot oven (400 degrees) for about 30-35 minutes. Remove from the oven and allow to cool for about 10-15 minutes to allow the meatloaf to solidify a little before attempting to cut slices.

Stuffed Bell Peppers
with an Italian Flavor

Prepare the Parmigiano Portabella Meatloaf recipe.

Directions:

Instead of baking a meatloaf, take 4 - 5 large sweet bell peppers, halve them and scrape out all of the seeds and white membrane. Spoon the meatloaf mixture into the pepper halves. Place in a shallow baking pan oiled well with olive oil. Pour a bottle of spaghetti sauce around the peppers, and dot the top of each pepper with a short piece of bacon or a sprinkle of Parmigiano cheese. Bake at 375 degrees for about 45 - 50 minutes.

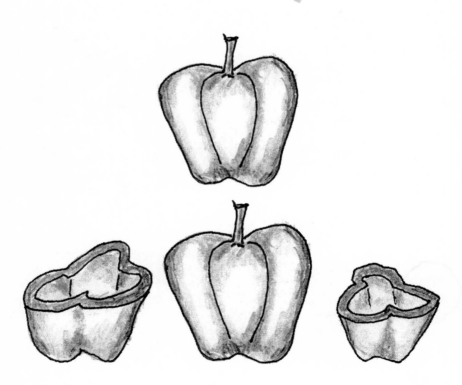

Venison Sausages

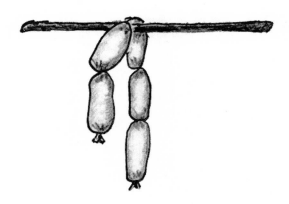

Venison Chaurice
Louisiana Grilling Sausage

Ingredients:

1 lb. boneless venison

1½ lb. boneless Boston Butt pork roast (aka "butts meat" in Charleston)

1 cup pork fat cut in ½" cubes (packed tight in cup)

1 medium onion grated finely

2 small cloves garlic, mashed completely & minced

2 tbsp. chili powder

1½ tsp. salt

½ tsp. fresh ground black pepper

1 tsp. sweet paprika

½ tsp. dried marjoram or thyme

3 - 4 tbsp. red wine

Directions:

Grind the venison and pork with a coarse plate on your grinder. Then, in a large mixing bowl pour in the mix of the spices & wine and mix thoroughly with the meat, kneading the sausage meat to blend. Using a pair of clean rubber kitchen gloves and mixing the meat with your hands is the best way.

Soak hog casings for a few minutes in tepid water in a coffee cup. Rinse the hog casings by running cold water through them like a hose for a few seconds. When they are pliable, thread them on the horn of the sausage stuffer, and load the stuffer with seasoned meat. Stuff the casings, and set out on parchment paper on a cookie sheet. Place the cookie sheet in the refrigerator overnight to let the sausage dry some on the outside, and to let the flavors marry.

In my experience in Louisiana, chaurice is typically not twisted into individual links. It is just put on the grill in long hanks, and then cut into servings after it is cooked. Brush the sausages with oil, and grill on the charcoal grill, or cook on a hot iron skillet.

Southern Plantation Venison Sausage

Ingredients:

1 lb. venison

1½ lb. boneless Boston Butt pork roast (aka "butts meat" in Charleston)

1 cup pork fat cut in ½" cubes (packed tight in cup)

3 level tbsp. Legg's #10 Old Plantation Pork Sausage Seasoning
   (in Chas. avail. at Doscher's Supermarket on Savannah Hwy. Comes in a bag with enough spices to make 25 pounds of sausage). Use exactly 1 tbsp./lb. ground meat. Note: Find all Legg's seasonings online at alliedkenco.com.

¼ tsp. cayenne pepper flakes (optional for hot sausage lovers)

3 - 4 tbsp. water

Directions:

Grind the venison and pork meat with a medium plate on your grinder. Then, in a large mixing bowl mix in the sausage spices, and water with the meat, kneading the sausage meat to blend.. Using a pair of clean rubber kitchen gloves and mixing with your hands is the best way.

Soak hog casings for a few minutes in tepid water in a coffee cup & run cold water through them like a hose for a few seconds. When pliable, thread on the horn of the sausage stuffer, and load the stuffer with seasoned meat. Stuff the casings, and set out on parchment paper on a cookie sheet. Place the cookie sheet in the refrigerator overnight to let the sausage dry some on the outside, and to let the flavors marry. If you don't have casings, just make bulk sausage with this recipe.

Brush the sausages with oil, and grill on the charcoal grill, or cook on a hot iron skillet.

Note: if unable to obtain Legg's #10 Seasoning, try this home made mix:

Spice Ingredients for 3 lbs. Southern Plantation Sausage:

3 tsp. Kosher salt

1 tbsp. rubbed dried sage (more or less to taste)

1 tsp. fresh medium ground black pepper

½ tsp. ground cayenne pepper

2 tsp. brown sugar

¼ tsp. ground ginger (optional)

¼ tsp. ground nutmeg (optional)

Mild Venison Butifarra Sausage

Ingredients:

1 lb. venison

1½ lb. boneless Boston Butt pork roast (aka "butts meat" in Charleston)

1 cup pork fat cut in ½" cubes (packed tight in cup)

3 level tbsp. Legg's #NS4 Sausage Seasoning
(available online at alliedkenco.com)

3 - 4 tbsp. white wine

Directions:

Grind the venison and pork meat with a medium or fine plate on your grinder. Then, in a large mixing bowl mix in the sausage spices, and wine with the meat, kneading the sausage meat to blend. Make sure to use the wine or the meat won't be soft enough to go into the casings easily. Using a pair of clean rubber kitchen gloves and mixing the meat with your hands is the best way.

Soak your hog casings for a few minutes in tepid water in a coffee cup. Rinse the hog casings by running cold water through them like a hose for a few seconds. When they are pliable, thread them on the horn of the sausage stuffer, and load the stuffer with seasoned meat. If necessary add a little more wine to make the mix soft enough to pass through the stuffing horn. Stuff the casings, and set out on parchment paper on a cookie sheet. Place the cookie sheet in the refrigerator overnight to let the sausage dry some on the outside, and to let the flavors marry.

Brush the sausages with oil, and grill on the charcoal grill, or cook on a hot iron skillet. Good with white beans.

Note: if unable to obtain Legg's #NS4 Seasoning, try this home made mix:

Spice Ingredients for 3 lbs. Mild Butifarra Sausage:

3 tsp. Kosher salt

½ tsp. sweet paprika

¾ tsp. fresh ground black pepper

½ tsp. ground cinnamon

¼ tsp. ground ginger

¼ tsp. ground nutmeg

Venison Beer Sausages
with a German Flavor

Ingredients:

1 lb. venison

1½ lb. boneless Boston Butt pork roast (aka "butts meat" in Charleston)

1 cup pork fat cut in ½" cubes (packed tight in cup)

4 lg. cloves garlic mashed completely & minced finely

1½ tsp. ground allspice

3 tsp. Kosher salt

1 tsp. fresh ground black pepper

2 tsp. sweet paprika

3 tbsp. beer

Directions:

Grind the venison and pork meat with a fine plate on your grinder. Measure all of the dry spices and salt into a small cup, and blend thoroughly. Set aside. Mash the garlic on a plastic cutting board or plate with a cooking knife, mince, and scrape up all of the garlic and put it in a cup. Add the 3 tbsp. of beer to the garlic and mix.

In a large mixing bowl with the ground meat, sprinkle the dried spices and salt evenly over the meat, and strain the garlic-infused beer through a fine sieve so all of the garlic juice and beer goes into the sausage meat. Mix well by kneading the sausage meat to blend all of the flavors completely. Using a pair of clean rubber kitchen gloves and mixing the meat with your hands is the best way.

Soak hog casings for a few minutes in tepid water in a cup. Rinse the hog casings by running cold water through them like a hose for a few seconds. When pliable, thread on the horn of the sausage stuffer, and load the stuffer with seasoned meat. Stuff the casings, and set out on parchment paper on a cookie sheet. Place the cookie sheet in fridge overnight to let the sausage dry, and to let the flavors marry. If desired, stuff the casings loosely, & pinch the sausage every 3 - 4 inches, & twist into links. Twist each link in an alternating direction, 3 turns left, and 3 turns to the right so they will not come undone.

Brush the sausages with oil, and grill on the charcoal grill, or cook on a hot iron skillet. Serve on a bun like a hotdog with good mustard and relish or with some minced onion and sauerkraut.

Smoked Paprika Venison Chorizo

Ingredients:

1 lb. venison

1½ lb. boneless Boston Butt pork roast (aka "butts meat" in Charleston)

1 cup pork fat cut in ½" cubes (packed tight in cup)

4 lg. cloves garlic mashed fully on cutting board & minced

4 - 5 tbsp. smoked Spanish pimenton (paprika)

3 tsp. Kosher salt

½ tsp. ground cumin (optional)

½ tsp. fresh ground black pepper

2 - 3 tbsp. water

Directions:

Grind the venison and pork meat with a medium or coarse plate on your grinder. Measure all of the dry spices and salt into a small cup, and blend thoroughly. Set aside. Scrape up all of the mashed minced garlic and put it in a cup. Add 3 tbsp. water to the garlic and set aside.

In a large mixing bowl with the ground meat, sprinkle the mix of the dried spices and salt evenly over the meat, and strain the garlic-infused water through a fine sieve so all of the garlic juice goes into the sausage meat. Mix well by kneading the sausage meat to blend all of the flavors completely. Using a pair of clean rubber kitchen gloves and mixing the meat with your hands is the best way.

Soak hog casings for a few minutes in tepid water in a cup. Rinse the hog casings by running cold water through them like a hose for a few seconds. When they are pliable, thread them on the horn of the sausage stuffer, and load the stuffer with seasoned meat. Stuff the casings, and set out on parchment paper on a cookie sheet. Place the cookie sheet in the refrigerator for 2-3 days to let the sausage dry out, and to let the flavors marry. If you have room, hang the sausage in the refrigerator to encourage drying.

Brush the sausages with oil, and grill on the charcoal grill, or cook on a hot iron skillet. Use this chorizo in rice dishes like paella or jambalaya, dried bean dishes like cassoulet, as an accompaniment or ingredient in egg dishes (omelets, frittatas, etc.), cooked in a frying pan with sweet peppers sautéed in olive oil, etc., etc. Very versatile sausage.

Fresh Venison Mettwurst

Ingredients:

1½ lb. venison

1½ lb. pork Boston Butt (aka "butts meat" in Charleston)

½ cup pork fat cut in ½" cubes, cup packed tight

1 tsp. sugar

3 tsp. Kosher salt

¼ tsp. ground allspice

¼ tsp. ground nutmeg

⅓ tsp. caraway seeds

⅓ tsp. ground coriander

⅓ tsp. dried mustard powder

⅓ tsp. Liquid Smoke (or omit if able to smoke the sausages)

¾ tsp. fresh ground black pepper

¼ cup beer

Directions:

Grind the venison and pork meat with a fine plate on your grinder. Or double grind with medium plate. Measure all of the dry spices and salt into a small cup. In a large mixing bowl with the ground meat, sprinkle the mix of the spices and beer into the meat. Mix well by kneading the sausage meat to blend all of the flavors completely. Using a pair of clean rubber kitchen gloves and mixing the meat with your hands is the best way.

Soak hog casings for a few minutes in tepid water in a cup. Rinse the hog casings by running cold water through them like a hose for a few seconds. When pliable, thread them on the horn of the sausage stuffer, and load the stuffer with seasoned meat. Stuff the casings loosely to allow the sausage to be twisted into links, and pinch and twist links every 4 inches, first to the right 3 turns, and then to the left 3 turns so the links will not come undone.

Set out on a cookie sheet for 2 - 3 days in the refrigerator to let the sausage weep and dry out, and to let the flavors marry. If you have room, hang the sausage in the refrigerator to encourage drying. Sautee or grill and serve with potatoes, cabbage, or on a bun with mustard.

Oil Funnel Black Pudding
with Chopped Pecans or Rice

After trying to use venison liver a number of the traditional ways of preparing liver, I've repeatedly found that it (like all liver) tends to get tough when cooked thoroughly. Even more tough than pork, veal, or chicken livers.

So in the quest to surmount that obstacle, I have developed a way of preparing it so it is tender and flavorful by emulsifying it in the blender with seasonings. The key to liver is the artful use of seasonings to complement its earthy richness.

Black pudding, blood pudding, boudin noir, morcilla, and sanguinaccio. All names for a sausage made from blood. In the South there is a preparation known colloquially as "liver pudding" which is traditionally made in a big iron kettle outdoors on "hog killing days". Liver pudding is thickened with corn meal. In the Lowcountry we also have a preparation made of organ meats called "rice pudding", and it contains... you guessed it, rice as the starch filler.

This sausage is technically not a blood pudding since it is based on liver instead of blood. However, the preparation is so similar, and it bears a striking resemblance to black pudding, so that is what I'm calling it!

In 1985 I toured England and Scotland with my friend Eric Nord after we both scraped an MBA out of UNC Chapel Hill. He was engaged to a young English doctor, and we visited her family in the north of England. One night I remember her father serving us "black pudding" with great pride. In Louisiana, while working in the offshore oilfield I encountered the Cajun version "boudin noir". Finally, on a family trip to Spain, in Girona, my son Henry and I went out one night together to a tapas bar, and had one of the most memorable nights of our trip. The show stopping tapa was "morcilla", a Spanish version of blood pudding studded with pine nuts.

This recipe separates the men from the boys. If you are throwing your venison livers to the dogs like most guys do, shame on you! Once you have your hog casings this recipe is so easy.

Note: If you don't have hog casings and you still want to try this, just butter a terrine, casserole, or large ramekin, pour the mix into it, and set the dish in another larger pan with ½ " of water, bake for 30 minutes, cool and slice into little brownie sized pieces. Serve on toast, on top of baked grits or polenta, or slice it and sauté in oil, then add to an omelet. Also good with cooked apples.

Ingredients:

1½ lb. venison liver sliced in ½" slices

3 - 4 strips thick cut smoked bacon chopped coarsely

1 lg. clove garlic

1 medium onion peeled and chopped coarsely

2 tsp. hot paprika or 2 tsp. sweet paprika & ¼ tsp cayenne

1½ tsp. salt

½ tsp. ground cinnamon

½ tsp. fresh ground black pepper

2 eggs

½ cup pecans chopped fine (or ¾ cup cooked white rice)

Hog casings

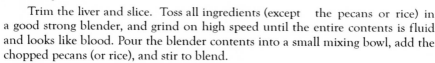

Directions:

Get a large saucepan of water simmering on the stove and season it with about 2 tsp. salt in a quart of water.

Trim the liver and slice. Toss all ingredients (except the pecans or rice) in a good strong blender, and grind on high speed until the entire contents is fluid and looks like blood. Pour the blender contents into a small mixing bowl, add the chopped pecans (or rice), and stir to blend.

Soak your hog casings to make them pliable, and cut off a piece about 24" long. Load your hog casings onto the spout of a large clean funnel (an oil change funnel works well). Take a rubber band and wrap tightly around the end of the hog casing nearest the cone of the funnel so it can't slip off of the spout when you start loading the casing with the fluid. Tie an overhand knot in the very downstream end of the hog casing that is hanging off of the funnel spout. Now you are ready to load the casing.

Have a helper hold the funnel above a dinner plate, and take your mixing bowl full of seasoned ground liver and pour it into the funnel, scraping to get every last bit! The casing will fill. Shake it a little to get the air bubbles to come to the top of the casing. While your helper is holding the sausage full of liquid, take short lengths of cotton kitchen twine and tie off short links of the sausage (about 3" each), making sure the fluid pressure in the casing is not too tight, or you may have your sausage explode while cooking!

When you are finished making links, tie off the last link with another overhand knot in the hog casing, or use string if you like. Place the tied black pudding links in the simmering water and gently poach for about 15 - 20 minutes until the sausages are cooked through. Do not boil or your sausages may explode. Pour off the hot water, and immerse the cooked sausages in an ice and water bath to rapidly chill them. Refrigerate until use.

Option:

For a Lowcountry "rice pudding" substitute ¾ cup cooked rice instead of the pecans. Add ¼ tsp. cayenne pepper flakes to the recipe depending on your taste for hot.

Note: Heinsohn's sells meat grinders & stuffers (www.texastastes. com). Northern Tool also imports sausage making equipment from China (www.northerntool.com). Get casings by asking your butcher.

Venison Soups

Neck Roast Borscht
in the Crockpot

This recipe is one reason you asked the butcher to save your neck roast. From a large deer, you can get 2 roasts large enough to use. From a small deer, just one. The roasts can be used whole, or cut into several thick slices with the butcher's band saw for use much like beef shanks.

The neck is a gnarly cut of meat with muscle fiber running in lots of different directions. Plan to cook it slow and long. This recipe utilizes a broth made in the Crockpot from the neck roast. Of course, the slow cooking renders the meat for the soup tender and delicious too! Making the soup involves two steps: (1) making the broth, and (2) assembling the rest of the vegetables that go into the soup.

Some folks say they don't like beets. Maybe it is just the strong color. If you think you don't like beets, then just think of borscht as vegetable soup and forget it has beets in it. You'll start to warm up to the idea of beets after trying this soup.

Broth Ingredients:

2 lb. venison neck roast (or 2½ lbs. venison ribs)

2 - 3 tbsp. cooking oil

½ onion-sliced

1 rib celery sliced into thin pieces

Handful of parsley stems

½ tsp. dried thyme leaves

6 - 8 whole black peppercorns

1 whole clove

1 tsp. salt

6 - 7 cups water

Broth Directions:

Put the Crockpot on the counter. Next place the oil in a deep skillet, and heat on medium heat. When hot, put the neck roast in and brown it on all sides. About half way through browning the meat, add the celery pieces, and onion. Arrange them around the meat, and allow the onions and celery to brown in the bottom of the pan without stirring them. Browning the vegetables is essential to creating the rich flavor and color we want in the broth. When the onions have caramelized, transfer the pan contents to the Crockpot. Add the parsley stems, peppercorns, thyme, and one whole clove to the crock pot. Use about 1 cup of the water to deglaze the frying pan, scraping the bottom, and then pour the hot contents into the Crockpot.

Put the rest of the water in a saucepan, and heat to boiling. Transfer the hot water into the Crockpot and put on the lid. Cook for 1-2 hours on high, then turn down the Crockpot to low, and cook the broth and meat overnight on low. The next day, turn off the heat, and allow to cool. Strain the broth, and discard all of the vegetables and spices. Next pick all of the meat off of the bones.

Soup Ingredients:

Prepare the broth and meat as outlined above

1 lb. beets-scrub, wrap in foil, & roast in oven 1 hour 'til tender

2 cups grated or finely sliced cabbage (green or red)

1 onion, chopped finely

2 carrots, peeled, and chopped

2 ribs celery, washed and chopped

3 - 4 peeled tomatoes-chopped, or one 16 oz. can tomatoes (chopped)

3 tbsp. tomato paste

2 potatoes peeled and cut into 1" cubes (optional)

2 tbsp. red wine vinegar or lemon juice

2 - 3 cloves garlic minced

1 tsp. sugar

1½ tsp. salt or to taste

Soup Directions:

Prepare the broth and meat as directed above. Turn the Crockpot up to high again, and add to it all of the vegetables listed in Soup Ingredients above. Remove the beets from the oven and allow to cool. When cool enough to handle, slip the skins off of the beets, and slice the beets into thin strips, then add them to the soup. Add the vinegar, sugar, tomato paste, tomatoes, garlic, and salt. Cook the soup in the Crockpot on high for about 1 - 2 hours or until all vegetables are tender. Ladle into bowls, and serve with a spoonful of sour cream added to each individual bowl of soup. Refrigerate and enjoy any left-over soup, or freeze for later use.

Shchi
Venison, Cabbage, Potato & Sauerkraut Soup

This recipe is Russian, and is another neck roast soup.   Like the preceding recipe, making the soup involves two steps: (1) making the broth, and (2) assembling the rest of the vegetables that go into the soup.

In the Russian language, which uses Cyrillic letters, the word for this soup is 2 letters long. In English it takes 5 letters to convey the sound. In German it takes 8 letters. So much for language economy!

Broth Ingredients:

2 lb. venison neck roast (or 2½ lbs. venison ribs)

2 - 3 tbsp. cooking oil

½ onion-sliced

1 rib celery sliced into thin pieces

Handful of parsley stems

½ tsp. dried thyme leaves

6 - 8 whole black peppercorns

2 whole cloves

1 tsp. salt

6 - 7 cups water

Broth Directions:

Put the Crockpot on the counter. Next place the oil in a deep skillet, and heat on medium heat. When hot, put the neck roast in and brown it on all sides. About half way through browning the meat, add the celery pieces, and onion. Arrange them around the meat, and allow the onions and celery to brown in the bottom of the pan without stirring them.   Browning the vegetables is essential to creating the rich flavor and color we want in the broth. When the onions have caramelized fully, transfer the pan contents to the Crockpot. Add the parsley stems, peppercorns, thyme, and whole cloves to the Crockpot.

Use about 1 cup of the water to deglaze the frying pan, scraping the bottom, and then pour the hot contents into the Crockpot.

Put the remaining water in the microwave oven in a large Pyrex measure or place it in a saucepan, and heat to boiling. Transfer the hot water into the Crockpot and put on the lid. Cook for about 2 hours on high, then turn down the Crockpot to low, and cook the broth and meat overnight on low. The next day, turn off the heat, and allow to cool. Strain the broth, to catch and discard all of the vegetables and spices. Next, pick all of the meat off of the bones, and return the meat to the strained broth in the Crockpot.

Soup Ingredients:

Prepare the broth and meat as outlined above

3 - 4 tbsp. butter

2 tbsp. flour (optional)

2 cups grated or finely sliced green cabbage

1 onion, chopped finely

2 carrots, peeled, and chopped

1 cup sauerkraut

1- 6 oz. can tomato paste

2 potatoes peeled and cut into 1" cubes

2 tsp. lemon juice

1 - 2 cloves garlic minced

1 Tsp. salt or to taste

Soup Directions:

Prepare the broth and meat as directed above. Turn the Crockpot up to high again. Sauté the vegetables (cabbage, onions, carrots) in the butter until wilted, and add to the soup in the Crockpot. (If a thicker soup is desired, make a roux by adding the flour to the butter and cooking it for a few minutes before adding the vegetables). Next add the sauerkraut and tomato paste along with the garlic, and salt. Cook the soup in the Crockpot on high for about 1 hour. Add the potatoes, and cook another hour or until all vegetables are tender. Ladle into bowls, and serve with a spoonful of sour cream and some fresh parsley leaves added to each individual bowl of soup. Refrigerate and enjoy any left-over soup, or freeze for later use.

Shredded Venison in Broth
with Winter Root Vegetables

Eating "in season" is gaining a lot of press, and rightly so. As I write this recipe, we are coming off of 14 continuous days of cold with hard freezes at night. This is rare in Charleston. "30% of Florida Fruits & Vegetables Damaged " the paper says. Is there any wonder people have been eating "roots" in the winter for millennia? Roots offer us a concentrated store of nutrients and vitamins to sustain us while the Earth rests and we plan the warm weather garden. This broth is based on root vegetables with some nice seasonings.

Ingredients:

2½ lb. venison neck roast (or 2½ lbs. venison ribs)

2 lbs. fresh venison marrow bones in 2" lengths (opt.)

1 onion peeled, halved & each half studded w. 2 whole cloves

2 tbsp. lard or vegetable oil

3 ribs celery diced

1 large white turnip or 3 small ones peeled and diced

3 carrots peeled and diced

6 scallions (green onions including tops) finely sliced

1 tsp. salt

10 cups water

1½ tsp. salt

¼ tsp. ground white pepper or ½ tsp. black pepper

Directions:

Put a large Crockpot on the counter and turn to high. Next, put all the water in a large saucepan and heat it on the stove, and keep it simmering to use later.

Heat the oil in a large nonstick skillet, and place the halved onions flat side down in the pan. Cook uncovered on medium until the flat underside of the onions are browned, but not burned (about 15-20 min.). Remove the onions and place in the Crockpot. If you have some, tie the onions in cheesecloth before placing in the soup so you can remove them at the end and discard the cloves. Otherwise, just toss them in as-is.

Next, sear the meat in the pan, browning it on all sides. Transfer to the Crockpot.

Add the diced carrots, turnips, and celery to the frying pan, and sauté for about 10 minutes until wilted, but not fully cooked. Transfer the vegetables to the Crockpot. Add the raw chopped scallions to the Crockpot. Add the salt and pepper also.

Ladle about 1 cup of the hot water out into the frying pan, and deglaze it completely. Add this pan liquid to the Crockpot, and then transfer the rest of the hot simmering water to the Crockpot, set on low, and cook the soup overnight, or leave on high and cook for 3-4 hours.

Remove the meat from the broth, separate it from the bone, chop, and return it to the soup. If using marrow bones, push the cooked marrow out of the short hollow bones, and return it to the soup. Remove the onion halves and discard the whole cloves.

Serve plain, or with a spoonful of sour cream, a squeeze of lemon, and a little chopped parsley on top.

If I Killed a Deer

Salads

Bartlett Pear Salad
with Cumin Pimento Cheese Dollop

If I haven't made it clear already, my grandmother Mary Stafford Baber Ellett was a very big influence on my cooking. I daresay, I gained my love of cooking from her. This salad is one thing she often put on the table when we visited in Myrtle Beach. Pretty simple, but mighty tasty!

The pimento cheese is influenced by Sam & Omie's Restaurant in Nags Head, NC. Spending time on the Outer Banks windsurfing, and such, Sam & Omie's had the best pimento cheese in the world! I finally sat there and decided why. It had a little ground cumin added to it. See if you don't agree!

Ingredients:
1 can Bartlett pears in juice or syrup (your choice)
1 bunch leaf lettuce, washed

Pimento Cheese:
1 block sharp cheddar grated
1 jar diced pimentos (including the juice)
½ cup mayonnaise
¼ tsp. ground cumin

Directions:
Set out several salad plates. Remove several of the outer leaves of the lettuce and dry them with a paper towel. Arrange a couple of pieces of lettuce on each salad plate.

Grate the block of cheese into a mixing bowl, and add the mayonnaise, pimentos, and cumin, and mix thoroughly.

Place a pear half on each salad plate with the lettuce, and using a teaspoon, put a large dollop of pimento cheese into the cavity of each pear. Sprinkle a small pinch of ground cumin on top of the pimento cheese dollop, and serve. If you like, also put a teaspoonful of plain mayonnaise on the top of the cheese dollop.

Red Grapefruit on Leaf Lettuce
with Honey Poppy Seed Dressing

Ingredients:

1 - 2 grapefruit(s)

Boston or green leaf lettuce to cover salad plates.

Directions:

Using a very sharp paring knife, cut the ends off of the grapefruit, and peel the grapefruit in a spiral fashion as you would an apple, just deeply enough to remove all of the white membrane covering the fruit sections. Next slip the blade of the knife down both sides of the membranes dividing the fruit sections, and remove the sections clean of any membrane. At the end, you will have a flimsy, ball of floppy grapefruit membrane dividers still attached at the center. Squeeze any remaining juice and then discard the membrane core.

Arrange the grapefruit sections in a fan shape on the lettuce leaves, spoon on some Honey Poppy Seed Dressing, and serve immediately.

Honey Poppy Seed Dressing

Ingredients:

¼ cup honey

3 tbsp. cider, rice, or red wine vinegar

2 tbsp. olive oil

1 tsp. poppy seeds

2 tsp. prepared Dijon mustard

1 tbsp. finely minced onion or scallion

Salt and fresh ground pepper to taste

Directions:

Mix all of the above ingredients together. Use on salads with fruit.

For example: Red grapefruit sections on a bed of green leaf or Boston lettuce.

Waldorf Weingelee
Wine Jelly Fruit Salad

This is a variation on the German dessert, wine jelly with fruit.

Growing up in the '60's both my mother and grandmother used to make various kinds of "congealed salads". They had an assortment of individual sized aluminum molds, and these small Jell-O-based salads often appeared on a bed of lettuce. The simplest rendition was orange Jell-O with a can of fruit cocktail mixed in.

This congealed salad is one step more sophisticated because of its use of white wine. I tried this combination because I like the crispness of the nuts, celery and apples, and the familiar combination of flavors of these traditional ingredients of the Waldorf Salad.

Ingredients:

2 crisp apples

1 rib celery

¼ cup raisins

¼ cup pecans or walnuts chopped

1 envelope Knox unflavored gelatin

1 cup dry white wine

1 tbsp. lemon juice

Scant ¼ cup sugar

¾ cup water

Mayonnaise (optional)

Directions:

In a small saucepan place the water, and sprinkle the gelatin into the cold water. Allow the gelatin to soften in the water for 2-3 minutes. Then set the saucepan on low heat and heat the water to just below a simmer, stirring and insuring the gelatin dissolves fully in the heated water. Pull the saucepan off of the heat, and add the sugar and lemon juice, and stir to dissolve the sugar fully. Next, add the white wine and stir to mix all of the liquid ingredients. Set the wine gelatin aside to come to room temperature.

When the wine gelatin has cooled, core the apples, and cut them into approximately ½" cubes, leaving the peel on the apple pieces. Chop the celery into approximately ¼" cubes. Chop the nuts. Combine the celery, apples, chopped nuts, and raisins in a bowl and set aside.

Using a Teflon lined nonstick muffin tin, fill each of the muffin tin compartments about ⅔ full with the apple-raisin-celery mix until you run out of the fruit mixture. The number of molds you are able to make depends on the size of the muffin tin. Pour enough of the wine gelatin mix into each of the muffin tin molds to cover the fruit. Put the muffin tin in the refrigerator for several hours or overnight to let the wine jelly set. When ready to serve, run a basin of warm water, and put the muffin tin down into the warm water for a few seconds to insure the gelatin next to the tin melts just a little bit. Place a large cutting board or cookie tin over the muffin tin, and turn it upside down and tap to help the wine jelly molds release.

Use a spatula to pick up the individual Waldorf Weingelee congealed salads and place one on top of a couple of leaves of green leaf lettuce or Boston lettuce arranged on individual salad plates. Top with a spoonful of mayonnaise.

Next time you make the wine jelly, adjust the sweetness to your liking. If you want it a little more tart use less water and more wine.

Moravian Cole Slaw

My wife Janice and I joined the Little Church on The Lane in Charlotte. It was a great little church, and very often we had covered dish meals after the Sunday service. It was a certainty that someone would bring this dish. Moravian Coleslaw is right up there with Moravian Chicken Pie, Moravian Sugar Cake, Moravian Ginger Snaps, and all of the other wonderful foods associated with the Moravian kitchen.

The Moravian Church is a pre-reformation Protestant denomination that traces its beginning to the martyrdom of Jan Hus, a Bohemian Catholic priest burned at the stake in 1415. It took 100+ more years before Martin Luther nailed his 95 Theses to the door of the Wittenberg Cathedral, setting off the Protestant Reformation in earnest. The formal name of the denomination is "The Unity of the Brethren".

The Moravian motto is "In essentials unity. In non-essentials liberty. But in all things love (which is charity)." The Southern Province of the church is centered in Winston-Salem, NC, and the Northern Province is based in Bethlehem, PA. The church publishes a daily devotional guide called The Daily Texts in 50 languages. Daily Texts are available on-line at: www.moravian.org/daily_texts/

Ingredients:

Brine: 2 c. water, 2 c. sugar, 2 c. white vinegar & 1 tbsp. salt

1 lg. head green cabbage about 3 lbs. grated finely

2 onions grated finely

1 large sweet green bell pepper grated finely

1 lg. carrot, peeled & grated finely

1 small jar pimentos finely chopped (opt.)

1 tbsp yellow mustard seeds

4 tbsp. cooking oil (optional)

Directions:

Heat the water, vinegar, salt and sugar in a non-reactive saucepan to boiling, and pull off the heat and let cool. Place cabbage, onion, green pepper, carrot, pimento (opt.), & mustard seeds in an earthen bowl.

When the vinegar brine is cool, pour it (and the oil if using) over the grated cabbage, onions, pepper and carrots, mix well, and cover. Refrigerate for 3-4 hours, or overnight. Improves with time in fridge!

Rote Rubensalat
German Style Pickled Beets

Another way to prepare pickled beets.

Ingredients:

2 lbs. fresh red beet roots boiled or roasted

Large sweet onion thinly sliced

Marinade:

½ cup red wine vinegar or cider vinegar

½ cup dry red wine

3 - 4 whole cloves

6 whole black peppercorns

½ tsp. ground coriander

¾ tsp. salt

Dressing:

3 tbsp. olive oil

1 tbsp. prepared horseradish

Directions:

Wash the beets with a soft brush, but try not to bruise them or break the skin to prevent bleeding during cooking. Place them unpeeled in a saucepan with enough water to steam them (about ¾" water). Cover the pan, and boil for about 40 minutes until fork tender. Add more water if needed to prevent scorching. Pour off the water and allow beets to cool, and then slip the peels off of the beets, and slice into ¼" slices. (Alternative, for more intense beet flavor, rub the skins with cooking oil, and place on foil in the oven to bake for 1 hour on 325 degrees. Remove beets from the oven and allow to cool, peel, and then slice as above).

Slice the onion into ⅛" thin slices. Combine the vinegar, wine, salt, along with the cloves, peppercorns, and coriander in a stainless saucepan, and bring to a boil. Add the sliced onions then pull off of the heat and immediately pour the marinade & onions over the beets. Let cool, cover and refrigerate overnight. Remove the whole cloves and peppercorns from the dish and discard them. Combine the olive oil and horseradish in a small bowl, and stir to mix thoroughly. Pour this dressing over the marinated beets, and turn to coat with the sauce. Serve alone or on a bed of lettuce.

Tomato Aspic Ring
with Buttermilk Blue Cheese Dressing

I dedicate this recipe to the late Jim Sanders of Atlanta, author of "Jim Sanders Cooks for Wine Lovers-and those poor souls who haven't yet discovered the glory of the grape". This small intimate book is part of my collection of cookbooks. Here is how I obtained it.

I had the pleasure of meeting Mr. Sanders at his wine shop in the Atlanta suburbs about 1999. He invited our small group of guys including Chris Branch and John Delaloye (who got us the invitation) into his inner sanctum where he offered tastes of his own imported French wines from Burgundy and the Beaujolais. While the normal customers came and went out in the shop, I will never forget sitting in the back with Mr. Sanders describing his Beaujolais Villages to us as his "constant companion". We sat in his back room for about 2 hours as he opened bottle after bottle of Burgundy including an annual fundraiser wine made for the Hospice de Beaune. And copious quaffs of all of the wines of the villages of the Beaujolais. Fleurie, Moulin a Vent, Chiroubles, etc., etc. Mr. Sanders bicycled through the French wine growing regions in 1948 and found his life's calling.

Mr. Sanders didn't cook for us unfortunately, so we all were thoroughly light headed by the time we went up front to make our purchases. I learned many things about wine here, including the fact that the Beaujolais wines are meant to drink now, not to store. I lost my head and bought too many bottles, and subsequently lost several bottles by keeping them for a couple of years.

So, Mr. Sanders has passed away, but there is some great biographical information on him at www.docsnews.com/invino.html.

Jim Sanders was a teacher and consultant to many, and they say he literally introduced fine wine to Atlanta, and by extension to the Southeast US. He was selected on 18 occasions for Confrerie des Chevaliers du Tastevin, awards presented by the prestigious French Burgundy fraternity. In 1986 the French government awarded Jim Sanders its Merite Agricole medal, France's highest award for a wine and food professional. Quite a rare achievement for an American!

Ingredients:

3 cups canned tomato juice or V-8

½ cup finely diced celery

2 tbsp. Worcestershire sauce

1 bay leaf

½ cup water

½ cup pimento-stuffed Spanish green olives sliced

½ cup finely diced onions

Juice of ½ lemon

1 tsp. Tabasco sauce

2 envelopes Knox gelatin

Pam cooking spray

Directions:

In a stainless saucepan, heat the tomato juice with the bay leaf & simmer 10 minutes and stir in lemon juice, Worcestershire Sauce, and Tabasco (or Balsamic vinegar). Stir 2 envelopes of gelatin into ½ cup of cool water and allow to dissolve. Add the gelatin to the tomato juice and turn off the flame. Allow to come to room temperature then add the minced onions, celery and olives and mix.

Pour the contents out into a non-stick Bundt cake pan that has been sprayed lightly inside with Pam. Refrigerate several hours or overnight without disturbing it. When ready to serve, run a couple of inches of warm water into your sink or a large bowl, and set the Bundt cake-pan mold down in the warm water for just a few seconds to melt just the outside layer of the gelatin so the aspic will come out of the mold easily. Cover the top of the Bundt pan with a large serving plate. Holding the whole affair together, next turn the cake-pan mold over and catch the aspic ring on the plate. Garnish with lettuce or parsley. Drizzle with Buttermilk Blue Cheese Dressing, and serve in slices. Keep the leftovers in the fridge for up to a week.

Buttermilk Blue Cheese Dressing

Ingredients:

4 oz. blue cheese

½ cup mayonnaise

¼ cup buttermilk

Directions:

Mash the blue cheese with a fork, then add the buttermilk and mayonnaise. Whisk to blend completely, and then serve with the aspic.

Tangy Potato Salad
Spiked with Okra Pickle Juice

Ingredients:

1½ lb. waxy boiling potatoes (not Idaho bakers)

1 medium sweet onion (Vidalia, Wadmalaw Sweet, etc.) diced

½ cup diced sour pickle (dill pickle, pickled okra, etc.)

½ cup mayonnaise

¼ cup okra pickle juice (Save juice when the pickles are gone!)

1 sweet red bell pepper roasted, skinned, seeded & diced

2 tbsp. Dijon or yellow prepared mustard

½ tsp. fresh ground black pepper

Directions:

Wash the potatoes and place them in salted water to boil. Boil for about 15-20 minutes. Test with a fork to make sure they are beginning to get tender, but are still firm and able to be sliced. We don't want the potatoes cooked to the point of crumbling. Drain the potatoes and set aside on a cutting board to cool. When cool, slip the skins off. Slice into ¼" thick slices.

In a mixing bowl, combine the mayonnaise, diced onion, diced pickle, sour pickle juice, ground black pepper, minced red bell pepper, and mustard. Whisk all of these together completely to form the dressing. It should be quite thin. This is ok, because the potatoes are going to soak it up much like a marinade.

Add the sliced potatoes to the dressing, and turn several times with a rubber spatula to coat all of the potatoes.

Serve at room temperature for the best flavor. Refrigerate the leftovers.

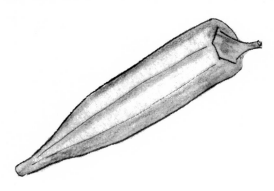

Vegetable Side Dishes

Braised Red Cabbage
with Green Apples & Onions

A good German inspired use of cabbage, great with game dishes in cool weather. This is a good example of "eating in season" which the current generation foodies have re-discovered and promoted as if it was a new concept. Cabbage and apples being fall crops, and onions being stored year-round, this dish comes to my mind when the summer eggplant, squash, peppers, and fresh tomatoes are just a memory. It is the season for roots and cole crops like cabbage.

Ingredients:

1 head red cabbage washed & sliced into thin strips like cut slaw

2 Granny Smith apples peeled, cored and julienned (very thin strips)

1 small to medium onion minced

2 - 3 strips of thick bacon cut in short pieces (or 2 tbsp. Butter)

¼ tsp. salt or ½ tsp. salt if butter is used instead of the bacon

2 - 3 tbsp. honey

2 - 3 tbsp. cider vinegar

Directions:

In a skillet, sauté the bacon pieces to render all of the fat. Remove the bacon from the grease, and set aside. Crumble when cool and reserve for later. Place the diced onion in the pan and sauté until the onion is wilted. Add the cut cabbage and apples to the onions in the bacon grease, and add a couple of tablespoons of water. Add the honey, vinegar, and salt. Put a tight lid on the skillet, and slowly braise the cabbage. Cook slowly enough to allow the cabbage to create its own steam. If needed occasionally put a couple of tablespoons of water to prevent scorching of the cabbage. The cabbage should however, wilt and caramelize through contact with the pan to develop its flavor. Braise cabbage like this for 45 minutes or until fully tender and reduced to resemble a nice pink marmalade-like consistency. Remove the lid, and raise the heat to make sure the cabbage does not have any extra liquid. Serve garnished with the crumbled bacon if desired, or finish with a pat of butter.

Note, the acid in the vinegar insures that the red cabbage pigment stays red. In the presence of a higher pH (base), this acid-base pigment indicator will turn blue. Watch for this to happen when you clean up and put some dishwashing detergent in contact with any of the leftover cabbage. Fascinating food science !

Pan Sautéed Sweet Potatoes
with Dark Rum Glaze

Ingredients:

1 lb. sweet potatoes

2 tbsp. canola oil

2 tbsp. butter

¼ cup brown sugar (more if you are a sweet tooth)

½ tsp. ground cinnamon

1 oz. Myers Dark Rum

Directions:

Peel the sweet potatoes. Slice them in half lengthwise. Halve crosswise. Dribble oil on the bottom of skillet. Arrange slices in skillet as tight as you can pack them in a single layer. Cover and cook on very low heat for 20 min. being careful not to burn. Cooked slowly they make a little of their own steam. Turn with spatula, add ¼ c. water or juice (orange or apple) & put the lid back on, and cook for 10 min. more. Remove lid & add sugar, cinnamon, rum, and butter. Cover, and heat through. Remove lid and cook for a few minutes if needed to concentrate the syrup. Spoon the sweet syrup in the bottom of the pan over the potatoes and serve. Good left over too!

Onions in Red Wine

Ingredients:

1 lb. whole small onions (or medium size, peeled and halved)

2 tsp. flour (or rice flour if gluten sensitive)

3 tbsp. butter	1 cup red table wine
½ tsp. salt	2 bay leaves
1 tsp. brown sugar	¼ tsp. ground allspice

Directions:

Put the butter in uncovered skillet & sauté onions about 10 min. Add the flour, and stir into the butter in the bottom of the pan, cooking for a few more minutes. Add salt & bay leaves along wine, & cover. Cook covered for about 20 min. Finish by adding sugar & allspice, & raise heat to reduce sauce & thicken it for about 5 min.

Jager Kohl
Hunter's Cabbage with Jagermeister

Around 1990 I visited my friend Tim Owen in Atlanta. I had never heard of Jagermeister, but it was popular in the bars in Atlanta then. Brilliant marketer and importer Sidney Frank had teamed up with the manufacturer, Mast-Jagermeister of Wolfenbuttel Germany. Mr. Frank noticed the New Orleans custom of serving cold shots of Jagermeister. So he introduced the Jagerettes, teamed up with band Metallica, and swept the US bar scene with a medicinal digestif made by cold infusion of 56 natural herbs and spices. It tasted good in Atlanta so I bought a bottle at home but couldn't drink it. Rather than throw it away I guessed the spice of Jagermeister might be an interesting combination with cabbage which is used a lot in German cooking. See if you agree.

Coincidentally Jagermeister ties right into the theme of this book. The term "Jagermeister" was coined in 1934 as a result of the new Reich Hunting Law. Senior foresters and game managers were dubbed "Jagermeisters". Jager means "hunter" and "meister" of course means "master" in German (not to be confused with the "jaeger" which was an early German sporting long arm with a rifled barrel, the inspiration for the American Pensylvania or "Kentucky" long rifle). The newly minted jagermeisters were employees in the German civil service. Jagermeister (the drink) went on to be used as a field anesthetic during WWII, which erupted soon after Jagermeister's debut as a medicinal in Germany.

The symbol of the stag with a beaming cross between its antlers recalls a young nobleman in Belgium's Ardennes forest. Enamored of the chase, instead of attending Good Friday mass, he went hunting. While pursuing a great stag it turned its head revealing the gleaming cross between its antlers, and God won a man to his service. Antlers, being shed and grown anew each year symbolize our renewal in God's grace, and that hunter became St. Hubert, bishop of Liege, and patron saint of all hunters.

Originator Curt Mast, a passionate hunter & outdoorsman, dedicated his herbal concoction to hunters and to their honorable tradition, On the side of the Jagermeister bottle is a little poem. When translated:

> *This is the hunter's badge of glory,*
> *That he protect and tend his quarry,*
> *Hunt with honor, as is due,*
> *And through the beast, to God be true.*

Ingredients:

1 head green cabbage washed & sliced into thin wedges

2 - 3 strips of thick bacon cut in short pieces (or 3 tbsp. butter)

½ tsp. salt

¼ tsp. fresh ground black pepper

1 tbsp. sugar

1 tbsp. cider vinegar

1 oz. Jagermeister Liquor

1 tbsp. flour (optional)

½ cup sour cream

Directions:

In a skillet, sauté the bacon pieces to render all of the fat. Remove the bacon from the grease, and set aside. Crumble when cool and reserve for later.

Place the sliced cabbage in the bacon grease, and add a couple of tablespoons of water. Put a tight lid on the skillet, and slowly braise the cabbage in the oil. Cook slowly enough to allow the cabbage to create its own steam. After about 10 - 15 minutes, add the salt, pepper, sugar, and vinegar (and flour if using). If needed occasionally put a couple of tablespoons of water to prevent scorching of the cabbage. The cabbage should however, wilt and caramelize through contact with the pan to develop its flavor. Braise cabbage like this for 30-40 minutes.

Remove the lid, and raise the heat to make sure the cabbage does not have any extra liquid. Finish cooking by adding the shot of Jagermeister, and cooking covered for another 10 min. on medium. Serve individual servings with a dollop of sour cream and garnished with the crumbled bacon.

Trinxat
Catalan Cabbage & Potato Pancake with Bacon

In the Spring of 2009, my wife Janice organized a trip for us to go to Girona (both a region within Cataluña, and a city), which is technically in Spain. Lance Armstrong and many elite cyclists live and train in and around the medieval city of Girona with access to the nearby Pyrenees.

Cataluña is a land divided among 3 countries (Spain, France & Andorra). The Catalan people have their own language, and they would prefer to be independent from either France or Spain. So, in some ways it is similar to South Carolina, which in spirit never fully rejoined the Union after our Civil War in 1865. Cataluña includes Barcelona in Spain, and Perpignan in France.

Catalan food preparation bears many influences that trace into the distant mists of time to the Medieval, Roman, and even further back in time. Some believe Spain has become the culinary epicenter of the world, taking that title away from France. In the seaside town of Roses, is the restaurant El Bulli run by Catalan chef Feran Adria'. It is widely accepted that El Bulli is the most difficult restaurant in the world to obtain a reservation. Adria's assistants work feverishly all winter in their Barcelona test kitchen (laboratory) concocting dishes for the next season. The restaurant opens for business each year in the summer high tourist season. Reservations are taken a year in advance.

Switching gears, this recipe is Catalan poverty fare from the high Pyrenees where pasture land is scarce, soil is thin, and the nights are cold. Trinxat is a vegetable dish using two vegetables that prefer to grow in high cold places. cabbage and potatoes.

The Catalan cuisine is known as a beefless cuisine because of the scarcity of pasture land for cattle grazing. However, pork, game, seafood, and vegetables prevail.

Trinxat means "chopped" in Catalan, and is pronounced "trinshat". The "x" in Catalan is pronounced 3 different ways, but in this case like "sh". The cabbage should be a late season winter cabbage touched by frost to insure it is the sweetest possible. Savoy cabbage is used in Europe, but our green cabbage works well for this too. The bacon should be good quality, thick-cut & dry-cured.

In our area, Meggett, S.C. just south of Charleston was famous in the early 1900's for producing huge amounts of cabbage and potatoes for the US produce market. Incorporated in 1905, Meggett was a boomtown, and the cabbage capital of the world. The town is situated on rich soil and had access to a spur of the Atlantic Coast Line Railroad and a large wharf on Yonges Island. A group of farmers banded together to form the South Carolina Produce Association brokering produce nationwide using ticker tape and the telephone lines. So this dish would be at home in Meggett!

Ingredients:

2 - 3 lbs. whole head of cabbage

2 lbs. boiling potatoes peeled

6 slices dry cured bacon

3 tbsp. virgin olive oil

1 clove garlic peeled, crushed & minced

Fresh ground black pepper

½ tsp. cumin seeds or ground cumin (optional)

Directions:

Take out a large saucepan with a lid. Place the potatoes in it and fill to half cover the potatoes with water. Add about ½ tsp salt. Boil the potatoes for 30 minutes or until tender.

Take the outer tough leaves off of the cabbage, cut the stem out by inserting a small paring knife and cutting it out so there is a 2" cone shaped hole in the bottom of the cabbage. Place the cabbage in a large pot with this hole side facing down, and add about 2 - 3 inches of water to the pot with 1 tsp. salt. Cover it, and boil the cabbage for 45 minutes or until very tender.

Turn both the cabbage and potatoes out into a colander or sieve, and allow them to drain and cool. Press on the cabbage to make sure it releases all of the water. Working in batches mash the potatoes coarsely with a fork or potato masher. Chop the cooked cabbage up well with a large kitchen knife on a cutting board. Combine the cabbage and potatoes in a large bowl. Mix and mash them together. This can also be done with a food processor, but make sure not to puree the vegetables. They should be coarsely chopped. Remember, trinxat means "chopped" in Catalan. Sprinkle in the cumin if you want to use it, mix well, and set aside the bowl of chopped vegetables. Fry bacon & remove from pan. Drain half the oil. Add cabbage-potato mix into the skillet and fry until brown on bottom. Run under broiler to brown the top. Lay cooked bacon slices on top, then serve the trinxat sliced like pizza.

Glazed Carrots
with Orange Juice & Candied Ginger

The carrots should not be cooked with salt.

Ingredients:
1 lb. carrots

½ cup orange juice

2 tbsp. honey

3 - 4 pieces of candied ginger (diced finely)

4 tbsp. unsalted butter

Directions:
Peel the carrots & trim the ends. On a cutting board, slice the carrots. Make a point to cut them on an angle of about 45% versus straight across the axis of the carrot's length. This makes for nicer, longer, slices with pointed ends. In a large saucepan, place the carrots along with the orange juice and the candied ginger pieces. Heat on medium high to get the carrots steaming and cover the saucepan tightly. Turn down to simmer and cook for about 10 minutes. Remove lid, and turn up the heat to medium high, and drive off the pan liquid through evaporation to reduce it down. Stir occasionally. The dish is done when very little liquid remains, and most of it coats the carrots. Finish by adding the butter, allowing it to melt, and stir. Serve hot.

"Geeched" Rutabaga
with Tomato, Onion & Smoked Meat

In the Lowcountry of South Carolina, you will often see a Gullah-Geechee vegetable dish that contains 2 vegetables and smoked pork "seasoning meat". This kind of vegetable combination is done with green bell pepper and cabbage. Also with okra and cabbage. Also with collards and rutabaga (See Gator Hut "Geeched" Collards). I believe this custom of cooking a couple or three vegetables with a little meat for long periods of time is of African origin. It is one pot cookery that is very West-African, and provides us a trace of the African kitchen here in the Lowcountry. You'll run across a number of these combinations. Whenever I cook any vegetables this way I call them "Geeched". You could call them "Gullahed" but "Geeched" seems to make a better verb.

Here is a "Geeched" way to prepare the waxed rutabaga. Rutabagas are ubiquitous in the stores around Charleston in the fall and winter.

Ingredients:

1 large waxed rutabaga peeled & chunked into 1" cube

3 tbsp. cooking oil

1 can whole or chopped tomatoes (15 oz.)

1 medium onion peeled and chopped coarsely

½ lemon, juiced

½ lb. smoked pork neck bone or brisket

½ tsp. salt or to taste

Fresh ground black pepper to taste

2 tbsp. butter

Directions:

Heat the oil in a large saucepan. Add the rutabaga and onion, and cook in the oil on medium for about 10 minutes until the onions are transparent, and the vegetables are steaming. Add the smoked pork, the can of tomatoes, the lemon juice, salt, and black pepper. Cover and stew until the rutabaga is fragrant and tender (about 1 hour). Stir the butter in at the very end of cooking. Serve. Save the leftovers and re-heat. This is even better the next day.

Gator Hut "Geeched" Collards

Ingredients:

2 large bunches collards & 1 small head cabbage chopped (optional)

1 waxed rutabaga

2 cups dry white wine

1 chopped onion

1 pound (or more) smoked ham, neck bones, or hocks.

2 - 3 tbsp. sugar

1 tbsp. salt depending on how much smoked meat is used

2 - 3 cups of water

Black pepper to taste

Directions:

Triple wash your collards using the immersion method. In other words, get your kitchen sink clean, and fill it with enough water to completely immerse your greens and agitate them like a washing machine would. This floats the sand off and you will feel it in the bottom of the sink. Remove greens, and rinse the sand down the drain. On the final rinse you should not feel any. If you do, then keep filling and draining until the greens are spic-n-span. Running greens under the tap water won't cut it. If you serve me greens with grit I'm not coming back to eat at your place next time!

Get a sharp kitchen knife and a cutting board. Take the heavy stems out of the collard leaves but leave your smaller inner leaves with the tender stems intact. Grab several leaves at a time, and roll them up like you were making a big fat cigar out of them. Start at one end and slice them off in strips about ½" thick. Make your way through all the stogies and put the julienned collards & cabbage in the pot. Peel the rutabaga and onion and chop them, and add to the pot. Rinse & brush off the smoked meat well to make sure it doesn't have any bone sawdust on it from the butcher shop. Add it to the pot. Add the wine, salt, sugar, and black pepper, and about 2-3 cups of water. Bring to a hard boil to wilt the greens. Add more water if needed to prevent scorching. If possible do this outdoors to keep from smelling up your house. I like the smell, but my wife can't abide it!

Take off lid and boil hard at the end, cooking the greens down until they are tender and re-absorb the liquid and are nearly dry. That's the Eastern NC way. Good collards should not leave a puddle on your plate!

Gratin of Turnips for Turnip Haters

This is the turnip recipe for people who say they don't like turnips. Justin Wilson had one similar to this, seasoned with parsley, red pepper and garlic powder. Here's my version.

Ingredients:

1 pound tender young turnips

2 large onions

3 eggs

2 - 3 tbsp. olive oil

¾ cup dry white wine

½ tsp. salt

Fresh ground pepper

¼ tsp. cayenne pepper flakes (optional)

Pinch of nutmeg

¾ cup grated Parmigiano or Romano cheese

¾ cup grated Swiss, Gruyere,
     or other flavorful white cheese

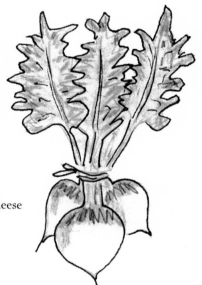

Directions:

Preheat the oven to 350. Peel the onion and slice very thin. Put sliced onion in one bowl. Peel the turnips and slice very thin. Put sliced turnips in a separate bowl.

Oil a shallow earthen casserole dish large enough to hold the ingredients.

Scramble the eggs, & add the wine and the salt and pepper to the eggs. Also the red cayenne pepper and the nutmeg if you are using those.

Beginning first with half of the sliced onions, put a layer of onions in the bottom of the casserole. Next, using half of the turnips, make a layer of turnips. Now sprinkle the turnips with the white cheese. Repeat a layer of onions using the remaining onions. Next a layer of turnips. Now pour the wine/egg mixture over the vegetables and let it perk down into the dish. Finally sprinkle the top with the Parmigiano cheese.

Bake for 1 hour on 350 degrees, or until the dish is browned on top, and fully cooked through. Allow to cool for 10 minutes before serving. This is really good re-heated the next day!

Sweet Celery and Apples

I frequently find a bunch of celery stays in the bottom drawer of the refrigerator for way too long. As a result, I'm always looking for a way to cook some celery as a stand-alone vegetable.

Ingredients:

1 lb. fresh celery stalks or hearts chopped

2 large cooking apples peeled and chopped

3 tbsp. butter

¼ tsp. salt

¼ cup sugar

1 cup white wine

Directions:

Wash the celery well and remove leaves. Chop into 1" lengths. Combine the celery, apples, butter, and salt in a nonstick skillet, and sauté until tender (about 20 minutes). Sprinkle in the sugar, then the white wine. Boil uncovered for about 10 minutes. Serve warm.

Apio
Lemony Celery

This is a recipe for celery from the Sephardim, the Jews of Portugal, Spain & Morocco.
I find it goes well with game and is a good way to use some celery up.

Ingredients:

2 lb. fresh celery stalks or hearts

1 cup water

Juice of 1 lemon

2 tsp. sugar (or honey)

½ tsp. salt

3 tbsp olive oil

Directions:

Wash celery, remove leaves & chop into 1½" lengths. Combine the water, lemon juice, oil, salt and sugar in a stainless saucepan and add the celery. Cover and boil for about 20 minutes. Serve hot, warm or chilled.

Sofregit
Caramelized Onions

Ingredients:

3 lbs. large onions, peeled and sliced thinly

¼ cup olive oil

Salt and fresh ground pepper to taste

Directions:

Heat the oil in a large deep skillet, Dutch oven, or large heavy bottomed sauce pan. Lay the onions down in the oil & cook for about 10 minutes until onions are wilted and beginning to turn golden. Continue to cook and stir occasionally.

It is ok to put a lid on it for a part of the cooking time, however, the final object is to reduce the onions down to a thick, sweet, rich marmalade-like consistency so the top must come off after the onions are wilted. The onions will actually begin to take on a waxy shine when most of the water is cooked off. The final amount of sofregit will only be about ⅓ to ¼ the volume of onions you began with in the pan.

Keeps well refrigerated. A spoonful of sofregit is delicious on a hamburger or cheeseburger cooked a la plancha. See the recipe for Hamburguesas a la Plancha. (pg. 67) Use left over sofregit in a cheese omelet.

Starch Side Dishes
Rice, Potatoes & Corn

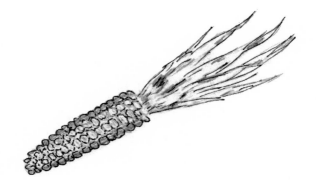

Long Grain Rice
Cooked "Proper"

Ingredients:

2 cups cold water

1 cup rice

½ tsp salt or to taste

Directions:

Pour salt & water into a large heavy bottomed sauce pan & bring to boil. Add rice, stir once to settle grains, but not again. Boil hard uncovered until small steam flutes bubble through the surface of the rice (about 7 - 8 min). Lower heat to a bare simmer & cover tightly with a well fitting lid or foil to get a good seal. Simmer 5 more minutes & turn off the heat. Don't lift the lid! Allow the rice to stand in the covered pot with lid on 'til 10 minutes have passed. Then lift the lid, and fluff with a fork

Cornmeal & Apple Muffins

Ingredients:

1½ cups fine cornmeal

1 peeled apple grated

¾ tsp. salt

3 - 4 tbsp. sugar

1½ cup buttermilk

2 - 3 tbsp. water if needed to loosen the batter

1 cup flour *

4 tbsp. canola oil

2 tsp. baking powder

2 eggs

*Gluten Free Opt.: subst. ½ c. rice flour, ¼ c. potato starch, 3 tbsp. tapioca starch & 1 tsp. guar gum or xanthan gum

Directions:

Spray muffin tin w. cooking spray & preheat oven to 350 degrees. In a mixing bowl, beat 2 eggs, & add buttermilk, grated apples & oil. Place the corn meal, salt, sugar, flour, and baking powder in a Ziploc bag & shake to mix. Pour the dry contents into the mixing bowl & stir quickly with a whisk. Fill the muffin tin with the batter and bake for 25 minutes.

Lowcountry Red Rice
Cooked Paella Style

Ingredients:

1¼ c. Carolina Gold (ansonmills.com), Arborio or med. grain rice

3½ cups chicken broth

3 - 4 tbsp. olive oil

Small onion chopped fine

½ green bell pepper, seeded and chopped fine

1 rib celery chopped fine

2 cloves garlic crushed and minced

3 tbsp. tomato paste

½ pound smoked sausage (or Venison Chorizo) in ½" thick rounds

½ tsp salt or to taste

2 tsp. sugar

Directions:

In a large heavy-bottomed non-stick skillet, brown the smoked sausage slices (if using Venison Chorizo -pg. 82 pre-cook an 8 - 10" link in a skillet then slice it into ½" rounds). Remove the meat from the pan, and pour off excess grease. Add the oil, and place all of the vegetables in the pan to sauté for about 10 minutes on medium, making sure onion is tender.

At this point, add dry rice to the sautéed vegetables and stir completely to coat the grains of rice with oil. Continue to cook on medium for another 3-5 minutes until the rice grains appear transparent on the outside with a core of pearly white color remaining in the center. Add the broth, tomato paste, sugar, salt and turn up the heat to medium high to reach a boil. Mash & stir to dissolve the tomato paste. Cook uncovered for about 5-8 minutes until the top of the rice appears dry above the liquid, with steam flutes visible up through the rice.

Quickly take the smoked sausage slices and arrange them by pressing them down individually in the rice like you'd arrange a pepperoni pizza in appearance. Cover the pan with a tight fitting lid or foil and turn to low to simmer on the stove top for an additional 12 minutes tightly covered. As an alternative, if you have the oven on, place the covered skillet in the oven to bake for 15 - 20 minutes on 350 degrees. Remove from the heat and allow to stand for 10 minutes before removing the lid. Ideally, the bottom should have a lightly browned, flavorful crust of rice. In Persian the crust is called the tadiq. In Spanish it is called the soccarat.

Risotto
with Mepkin Abbey White Oyster Mushrooms

After producing eggs for 40 years, the Cistercian monks of Mepkin Abbey began growing mushrooms in Moncks Corner, SC. Check out the fascinating clip showing how at: youtube.com/watch?v=CaqlPglJueE

My own experience includes growing shitake mushrooms in our back yard using sweetgum logs cut in the very early Spring, just before budbreak.

Ingredients:

1¼ c. Carolina Gold (avail. ansonmills.com) or Arborio rice

2 tbsp. extra virgin olive oil

½ tsp. salt & fresh ground black pepper to taste

2 tbsp. butter

Med. onion, finely minced

1 clove garlic peeled and sliced in thin slices

1 cup finely chopped White Oyster Mushrooms (or reg. white mushrooms)

½ cup white table wine

½ c. cream (opt.)

4 cups chicken,beef,or venison broth simmering in a saucepan

½ c. fresh grated Parmigiano cheese

Directions:

On medium melt the butter. Stir in the minced onion and cook gently until translucent and starting to turn golden (5 - 8 min.). Add the mushrooms, and sauté until wilted and liquid is all re-absorbed into them. Add the oil and salt, and then add the rice. Stir it and coat all of the grains with the oil and butter. Cook for a few minutes. This is what Italians call the "tostatura" step in making the risotto. It helps prepare the outer layer of the rice for the addition of the liquid. Now add the wine and cook on medium until all of the liquid is absorbed by the rice grains. I call this the quenching step. Next add the hot broth in stages. First 1 cup, stirring constantly if using Arborio. Don't stir if using Carolina Gold. Don't cover at any point. When the rice absorbs most of the moisture, add some more hot broth. Continue cooking for about 15 - 20 minutes so rice develops a creamy consistency on the outside, but still has a little firmness remaining to the bite on the inside of the rice grains.

Remove from the heat and stir in the grated cheese, and heat through for 2 - 3 minutes. Add a final ½ cup hot broth or cream and stir it in to give the dish a creamy consistency. Cover and allow to rest just a few minutes before serving. Sprinkle top with Parmigiano cheese if desired.

Glenn's Carolina Gold Risotto Milanese
Saffron Risotto

Spring 2009 I had the great pleasure of meeting Glenn Roberts of Anson Mills in Columbia, SC. He invited me to lunch with Dr. David Shields, USC's McClintock Professor of Southern Letters to discuss the wine I make from my Williamsburg Co. Norton/Cynthiana grapes, but that's another story. Glenn is taking the preservation and knowledge of landrace grains to a new level, and SC is so fortunate to have him. He is following his bliss, and is on a true quest! I include this recipe to call attention to Glenn's important work. Check it all out ansonmills.com.

Ingredients:

1¼ c. Carolina Gold (avail. ansonmills.com) or Arborio rice

Small onion, very finely minced

2 tbsp. extra virgin olive oil

2 tbsp. butter

½ cup white table wine

4 cups chicken broth simmering in a saucepan

¼ tsp. saffron threads placed in the simmering broth

½ c. fresh grated Parmigiano cheese

½ c. cream (opt.)

½ tsp. salt

Directions:

On medium melt the butter. Stir in the minced onion and cook gently until translucent and starting to turn golden (5 - 8 min.). Add the oil and salt, and then add the rice. Stir it and coat all of the grains with the oil and butter. Cook for a few minutes more on medium. This is what Italians call the "tostatura" step in making the risotto. It helps prepare the outer layer of the rice for the addition of the liquid. Now add the wine, and cook it on medium until all of the liquid is absorbed by the rice grains. I call this the quenching step. Next add the saffron infused hot broth in stages. First 1 cup, stirring constantly if using Arborio. Don't stir if using Carolina Gold. When the rice absorbs most of the moisture, add some more hot broth. Continue cooking for about 15 - 20 minutes so rice develops a creamy consistency on the outside, but still has a little firmness remaining to the bite on the inside of the rice grains.

Remove from the heat, stir in the grated cheese, the extra butter, and heat through for 2 - 3 minutes. Add a final ½ cup hot broth or cream and stir it in to give the dish a creamy consistency. Sprinkle top of each serving with Parmigiano cheese if desired.

Miss Ellett's Home Economics Spoon Bread
"Batter Bread" or Cornmeal Soufflé

This recipe is one of my Grandmother's old home economics standards. One of her first teaching assignments was in Wise County, Virginia. Wise County is hard up against the Kentucky line, and one might say, it is in "deeeeep Appalachia".

In the 1920's it was very fashionable for ladies to wear furs made of whole animal pelts, including sables, martins, etc. This was the "flapper" style! My Grandmother Mary Baber Ellett was quite fashionable, and she had a set of Russian Sables that I still own. They are fascinating to kids because they have beady little eyes, and they are put together with one sable catching the next sable by the tail in its mouth, forming a long string of furs to be worn like a scarf. I am sure that furs came in handy in the Appalachian winter. I remember hearing a story many times about one of her experiences with her class in Wise County. The first day she wore her Russian Sables to school, she walked in the classroom, and one of the teenage boys walked up and stroked the fur affectionately, and said in a proud Appalachian drawl, "They's monkeys ain't they, Miss Ellett?"

On their album "Not for Kids Only" Jerry Garcia and David Grisman recorded this traditional Appalachian song called "Three Men Went a Hunting". It gives a look into life and ethnicity in and around Wise County where the town of Norton, Virginia is located.

Three men went a-hunting
And something they did find
They came upon a porcupine
And that they left behind
The Irishman said it's a porcupine
And the Scotsman he said nay
The Welshman said it's a pin cushion
With the pins stuck in the wrong way

Three men went a-hunting
And something they did find
They came upon an outhouse
And that they left behind
The Irishman said it's an outhouse
The Scotsman he said nay
The Welshman said its a church house
With the steeple blown away

Three men went a-hunting
And something they did find
They came upon a toad frog
And that they left behind
The Irishman said it's a toad frog
And the Scotsman he said nay
The Welshman said it's a jay bird
With the feathers worn away

Three men went a-hunting
And something they did find
They came upon Norton
And that they left behind
The Irishman said it was Norton
The Scotsman he said nay
The Welshman said it's the end of the world
Let's go back the other way

So, why spoon bread has fallen out of favor is a mystery. If it was called what it really is, it probably would come back in style. It really is an elegant cornmeal or polenta soufflé wearing a down-home moniker. I can't think of a dish that connects the dots between the past and the present better than this one does.

Ingredients:

3 cups whole milk

1 cup fine cornmeal*

3 egg whites

3 tbsp. butter melted

1 tsp. salt

3 egg yolks

⅛ tsp. cream of tartar (optional)

*find some real artisinal meal @ ansonmills.com

Directions:

In a large saucepan bring the milk to a simmer and scald it.   Add in the cornmeal a little at a time, whisking to prevent lumps. Increase the heat to cook the mush until thick, about 5 minutes. Stir in the butter to melt and blend it with the mush by stirring. Remove from heat and allow to cool for 10 - 15 minutes. Stir a few times to encourage cooling.

Beat the egg yolks with ½ cup milk or cream. Add a few tablespoons of the corn mush to the eggs mixture and stir it together to temper. Then gradually add it all to the mush mixture, stirring constantly to blend the egg yolks in thoroughly.

Beat the egg whites with the cream of tartar until they just form stiff peaks. Mix the egg whites into the cornmeal mush mixture, blending thoroughly.

Pour the mixture into a very well oiled thin-walled earthen baking dish with straight sides. Dot the top with 5 - 6 pats of butter. Bake uncovered in the oven at 375 degrees for about 40 minutes. The top should puff up impressively like a soufflé, and it should be a nice brown color. Don't even think about opening the oven at any time during baking. Don't try to bake it while you are using the oven for other cooking either. You want the dish to puff, and disturbing it during cooking is a recipe for it to fall. Just watch it through the oven window. A knife or pick inserted should come out clean with no batter stuck to it when the soufflé is done. Serve immediately with lots of butter melted on top.

Option:

Add 1 cup of finely grated sharp cheese to the mixture just before adding the egg whites. Bake the same way. Result is delicious cheese soufflé.

Basic Polenta
or Grits

I bought a risotto/polenta spoon made from olive wood in Orvieto. You can get a solid maple or cherry one made in the USA from Harry at Kitchen Carvers (www.kitchencarvers.com). Harry's quality is extremely high. The spoon has a flat angled bottom with a large hole drilled right in the center of the spoon to allow the liquid to pass through as you stir. This avoids setting up a wave in the pot when you stir. It is very effective for cooking risotto, polenta, or even grits!

Ingredients:

1 cup yellow polenta (find artisinal polenta @ ansonmills.com)

4 - 5 cups water or chicken broth

½ tsp salt (if using water, none if using prepared broth!)

2 tbsp. butter

Directions:

Heat the water or broth to boiling. Gradually dribble the polenta into the boiling broth in a small stream, constantly stirring to prevent lumps. Cook on medium, stirring often to prevent sticking and scorching on the bottom. Continue to cook until the grains of corn polenta are fully gelatinized. There should be no tooth or crunch left in them, just smooth and creamy. Cooking time depends on polenta variety and grind.

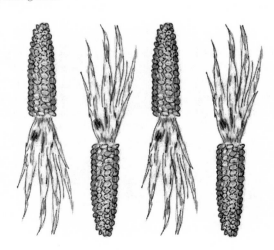

Baked Polenta (or Grits)
Topped w. Cheese & Sausage

Christmas 2007 my wife Janice set up a wonderful 2 week stay for us in Umbria. We spent most of it in the medieval hilltop town of Orvieto. We ordered this dish several times at a restaurant in our neighborhood. Orvieto is famous for its beautiful Duomo (cathedral). It is on a hill of solid tuffa (volcanic rock) that is very fragile as a result of all of the caves, wells, and basements that have been dug throughout its human occupation since Etruscan times. Orvieto and many of the other Tuscan and Umbrian hilltop towns were spared the destructive WWII bombing that was aimed at the industrial and rail locations in Italy. Arezzo and Foligno were not so lucky.

The first Allied bombing of Rome occurred on May 16, 1943. Immediately Pope Pius XII wrote US President Roosevelt asking that Rome "be spared as far as possible further pain and devastation, and their many treasured shrines from irreparable ruin." Roosevelt answered "Attacks against Italy are limited, to the extent humanly possible, to military objectives. We have not and will not make warfare on civilians or against nonmilitary objectives". Thank you Mr. Roosevelt.

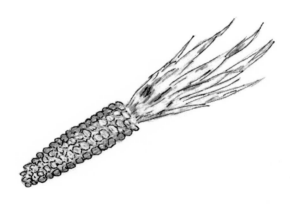

Directions:

Cook the polenta (or grits) as indicated previously. When done, turn out into a shallow baking dish or ramekin heavily oiled with olive oil. Cover the top with grated Manchego, Swiss, Asiago, or other flavorful white cheese. Next, sauté some crumbled sausage. Sprinkle the top of the polenta and cheese with the cooked crumbled sausage. Bake in the oven for 15 minutes on 400 degrees to heat through and to melt the cheese. Serve hot.

Millas
Pan Fried Slices of Polenta or Grits

Grits are called hominy in Charleston, but that is another story. This recipe is French, and can be made with either cooked grits or polenta. Some of the best around of either can be purchased on line from Anson Mills in Columbia (ansonmills.com). In the Southeast US white grits are preferred over yellow. Growing up in North Carolina, I always heard yellow corn was for the hogs. In Tuscany & Umbria yellow corn is preferred. Corn was poverty fare and many of the peasants there subsisted on corn polenta and chestnut flour versus the wheat-based pasta we now associate with Italy. Corn transformed agriculture, and so great was their dependence on corn in the diet that pellagra ran rampant. When corn came to Italy they did not know how to treat the corn with lime the way it was done by the Native Americans. Treating corn with lime unlocks the niacin and gains its full nutritional value.

Ingredients:
3 - 4 cups of hot freshly cooked polenta or grits (Pg. 126)
3 - 4 tbsp. corn starch (opt.)
Butter

Directions:
Make enough polenta to have left-overs. If making polenta or grits specifically for millas, you can add 3 - 4 tbsp. of corn starch to the pot of gruel to insure it will coagulate very well when the cooked corn cools. Make sure the grits or polenta are completely gelatinized. There should be absolutely no crunchy particles. Grits and polenta are NOT to be cooked al-dente.

Oil the inside of a Pyrex bread pan with soft butter. While the polenta is still hot and fluid, pour into the bread pan to fill it half way (about 2" deep). Place the pan on a rack & let the hot contents cool. When room temperature, place in the refrigerator with a kitchen towel over the top and leave for several hours or overnight to completely set up like Jell-O.

Unmold the solidified block, cut it into slices about ¾" thick. Fry the sliced millas for about 10 minutes on each side in butter or oil, making sure they begin to brown a little on each side. The outside should be crispy and the inside tender. Serve millas as a starchy side dish instead of pasta, rice or potatoes.

Potatoes & PET Milk Dauphinois

Who keeps cream in the fridge anymore? Try PET or Carnation condensed milk on this traditional French way of preparing potatoes.

Ingredients:

1½ lbs. potatoes peeled and sliced thin

1 can PET or Carnation condensed milk

¼ c. water

1 clove garlic

2 - 3 tbsp. softened butter

Generous pinch of nutmeg

¼ tsp. black pepper

¾ tsp. salt

Paprika (optional)

1 cup grated Swiss, Jarlsberg, or Gruyere cheese

Butter

Directions:

Halve the garlic clove, mash, and rub the inside of an earthen baking dish with it to coat with the garlic oil for flavor. Next rub the inside of the dish with the softened butter, coating it heavily.

Combine the potatoes, canned milk, water, salt, black pepper, and nutmeg in a large saucepan, and bring to a boil. Boil for 5 minutes, turning potatoes to prevent scorching. Transfer the mixture to the earthen baking dish.

Tamp down the potatoes, and sprinkle the top with the grated cheese. Dot with several more pats of butter. Sprinkle with paprika or hot paprika if desired. Bake at 350 degrees for about 40 minutes until the top is bubbly and golden brown.

Option:

Instead of PET or Carnation condensed cow's milk, substitute a can of Meyerberg's condensed goat's milk and top it off with some crumbled goat cheese (chevre).

If I Killed a Deer

Pickles & Conserves

If I Killed a Deer

Abandoned Farm Hard (Kieffer) Pear Relish

When you are hunting on an old farm in the South, often there will be an old pear tree somewhere around the old home site. These are not sweet eating pears. They are cooking pears, mostly known as Kieffer Pears. Coincidentally, in South Carolina's Lowcountry it is exactly the right time to harvest them when deer season starts mid-August. I can ride down the road in late summer and pick out the Kieffer pear trees from hundreds of yards away just based on their distinctive shape. This time of year the limbs are groaning with heavy fruit. Often the wise owner will prop planks up under the lower limbs to keep them from breaking under the weight of the fruit. Sometimes you can find these pears at one of the local farmers markets too, but don't hesitate, the season is quite short. This sweet relish goes well with most any kind of meal.

Ingredients:

10 - 12 lbs. hard (Kieffer) pears peeled, cored & chopped

2 lbs. onions (chopped)

3 green bell peppers chopped

3 red bell peppers chopped

6 cups white vinegar

5 cups sugar

2½ tsp. salt

2 tbsp. pickling spices tied in cheesecloth or a coffee filter

¼ cup sliced fresh ginger root (optional)

Directions:

Put the vinegar, sugar & spices in a large non-reactive pot and boil for 10 minutes with the lid off. Add the pears, onions, and peppers, bring to a boil as quickly as possible, and cook for about 10 minutes once it starts boiling. Immediately remove from the heat. Pull the spice bag out and discard it. Drop a piece of fresh ginger into the bottom of each jar, spoon the relish into sterilized jars, and top up with the vinegar sugar syrup to leave about ⅜" of airspace. Seal quickly with canning lids. If you plan to keep for a long time, you can process in a hot water bath for 10-15 min., but the acid content of this is such that it will keep well without doing that.

Pickled Okra
with Smoked Serrano Pepper & Garlic

Ingredients:
5 - 10 lbs. fresh okra
Quart jars or pint jars and lids
Brine proportions: 2 c. white vinegar, 2 c. water, & ¼ c. salt
Mustard seed (½ - ¾ tsp. per pint or 1 or 1½ tsp./qt.)
Calcium chloride (Pickle Crisp) ½ tsp./pint or 1 tsp./qt.
Peeled garlic cloves
Whole dried smoked Serrano peppers

Directions:
Wash okra. It is OK to trim the stems if they are long, but don't cut the stem entirely off. The seed chambers should remain fully enclosed by the stem end of the okra pods. Put a layer of your washed raw okra in each jar, stem side down with the points up. Then pack in a layer of pods with the points down. Pack each jar as tight as possible without bursting the pods. Take a packed jar and fill it to within ¼ inch from the top with water. Now pour the water out of the jar into a measuring cup. This measured amount of water shows you how much brine you will need for each jar. Multiply the measured amount by the number of packed jars of okra you have. Using this computation as a guide, make up enough brine to fill the jars plus a little extra. Make sure to use pickling or Kosher salt. Heat up the brine to boiling in a non-reactive (stainless steel) pot. Make sure your utensils, pot, and jars are squeaky clean because any oil or contaminants can cause your pickles to be mushy.

Set a roaster pan on the stove about half full of water, and get it boiling. Into each okra-packed jar, now place your Calcium Chloride, 1-2 smoked peppers, 1-2 peeled cloves of garlic, and the mustard seeds. Next dip the brine out of the simmering pot with a Pyrex cup, and fill each jar to about ¼ inch from the lip. You must fill the jars quite full, because the okra pods contain some air between the seeds, and most of that will get released during cooking and during storage.

Put the lids on and lightly screw on the rings, only 2 fingers tight. Place the jars in the roaster pan, and process in a covered boiling water bath for 15 minutes. Remove the jars from the bath and tighten the rings a bit as soon as they come out of the bath. Allow the jars to cool. Store 2 weeks before using.

Half-Sour Dill Pickles

Ingredients:
8 lbs. fresh pickling cucumbers (3 - 4" long)
Quart or pint jars and lids
Brine: 4 c. white vinegar, 12 c. water, & ⅔ c. Kosher salt
Black peppercorns whole
Calcium chloride (Pickle Crisp) ½ tsp. per pint or 1 tsp. per qt.
1 Dozen peeled garlic cloves
Dozen sprigs fresh dill weed (with seed heads)

Directions:
Wash the cucumbers and scrub with a vegetable brush. Cut a thin sliver off of the blossom end to prevent the pickles from being mushy. In a large stainless steel pot combine the vinegar, water, and salt and bring to a boil. Pack the cucumbers into sterilized jars. Drop a couple of garlic cloves, 3 - 4 peppercorns, and a sprig of dill in each jar. Put ½ tsp. (Calcium Chloride) in pint size jars. In qt. jars, 1 tsp. Calcium Chloride.

Fill jars with hot brine, and place the lids on without tightening. Place the jars of pickles in a water bath so the water is about half way up the sides of the jars, cover and process for 12 - 15 minutes in the boiling water bath. Tighten lids, and allow to seal as the jars cool on the counter.

Green Tomato Microwave Mostarda

This is a good way to use some of your green tomatoes picked before first frost. Back in May I bought an heirloom tomato plant called Sarah Black when I picked my son Henry up from The Asheville School where he is a boarding student. I planted it in the front yard and it produced a beautiful green vine larger than any tomato I ever have grown. Not a yellow leaf! All summer that tomato bloomed and dropped blossoms. The Charleston nights were too hot, and it did not set the first fruit. Then, as the days shortened, and the nights cooled a little in August, voilla, I began to have little tomatoes. In September they began to enlarge, and in October they ripened with beautiful pink bottoms and green caps with dark stripes. Luscious buttery flesh with lots of nice acid! I have saved plenty of seed, and now I know Sarah Black is what is known as a "late season" tomato. Just before Thanksgiving we still had green tomatoes, so they went into this mostarda.

My first encounter with this unique Italian condiment was the Christmas we spent 2 weeks in Venice in 2006. The stores carry little tubs of Mostarda di Venezia made from melocottone (quince). They serve it with bollito misto (boiled dinner of 7 meats served with 7 condiments). So, this green tomato mostarda is listed as a garnish for our Corned Venison Boiled Dinner!

Think of mostarda as candied fruit in a heavy syrup flavored with mustard. The name is from the Italian "mosta" which is grape must. Grape must, the sweet juice of raw grapes, was used for the syrup to candy all manner of fruit. Now we use granulated cane sugar to candy the fruit, as the base of the syrup. Lemon is nearly always included for acidity, and the lemon peel also is included for a little bitterness.

Ingredients:

2½ lb. green tomatoes

1 Charleston grown Meyer lemon (or reg. lemon)

1 lb. granulated sugar (2¼ cups)

3 - 4 tbsp. powdered Coleman's dry mustard

2 - 3 tbsp. white wine

Directions:

Wash tomatoes, and cut into chunks. Juice lemon, and remove all white membrane from the rind using a paring knife. Chop the rind coarsely. In a porcelain mixing bowl combine tomatoes, sugar, lemon juice, and lemon rind. Allow to sit & macerate (soak) for 4-6 hours. The fruit will give up its juice just like pouring salt on a slug. Pour mixture through a sieve to separate fruit & syrup. Collect syrup in a large Pyrex mixing bowl.

Place the mixing bowl of syrup in microwave on high, and cook until it boils up. As soon as it boils vigorously, open the door, and add the tomatoes to the syrup. Crank up the microwave again until the syrup boils up around the tomatoes for 5 minutes. Remove from the microwave, and again pour the tomato mixture through a sieve to separate fruit and syrup. Collect syrup in the same Pyrex mixing bowl. Set the tomatoes aside.

Return the mixing bowl full of only syrup to the microwave and boil it hard, watching it to prevent it from bubbling over the top. Also, don't overcook it. It should not be caramelized in the least. Expect your syrup to foam up nicely in the Pyrex bowl into a mound of clear frothy bubbles. Cook the syrup until it is the consistency of pancake syrup. If you have a candy thermometer, it should be "string stage" about 230 - 235 degrees. When syrup is reduced to that point remove & let it cool.

When cool, add back tomatoes and allow them to sit in the syrup for another 4-6 hours, or overnight. Cover bowl with a clean kitchen towel (not plastic wrap!). This should finish extracting most of the remaining water from the fruit. This thins down your syrup again. Now the tomatoes are on the way to being candied into mostarda. The tomato chunks should be very shrunken in size compared to their original size.

Again pour the tomato mixture through a sieve to separate the fruit and syrup. Collect the syrup in the same Pyrex mixing bowl. Put syrup by itself back in the microwave for the last cooking. Boil to the same "string stage" of 230-235 degrees, about the thickness of pancake syrup. Remove from microwave and let syrup cool fully. Then, pour the cooled syrup back in the tomatoes. Mix the mustard in with white wine to form a thin paste and pour this mustard paste into the mostarda. Stir completely to mix. Put the mostarda into jars and seal. Mostarda is not hot processed like a canned item. It is just packed in jars. The sugar content is so high that it is not susceptible to spoilage, but you can keep it in a cool place or the refrigerator if you like.

Pumpkin Microwave Mostarda

Think of mostarda as candied fruit in a heavy syrup flavored with yellow mustard powder. The name is from the Italian "mosta" which is grape must. Grape must, the sweet juice of raw grapes, was used for this syrup to candy all manner of fruit. Now we just use granulated cane sugar to candy the fruit, and to form the base of the syrup. Lemon is nearly always included to give us a little acidity, and the lemon peel also is included for a little bitterness.

Nearly any fruit can be turned into mostarda, and different places in Northern Italy each have their own characteristic mix of fruits, Cremona, Mantova, Venezia, etc.

See if you don't agree mostarda is magical stuff once you learn to make it!

Ingredients:

2½ lb. peeled pumpkin or butternut squash cut ¼" thick strips

1 Charleston grown Meyer lemon (or reg. lemon)

2½ cups granulated sugar

3 - 4 tbsp. powdered dry mustard

2 - 3 tbsp. white wine

Directions:

Wash the pumpkin, cut into slices, remove the seeds, and peel it deeply. Then cut pumpkin into strips about ¼" to ⅜" thick. Juice the lemon, and remove all of the white membrane from the rind using a paring knife. Chop the rind coarsely. In a porcelain mixing bowl combine the sliced pumpkin, sugar, lemon juice, and lemon rind. Allow to sit & macerate (soak) overnight at room temp. Pumpkin will release some of its juice just like pouring salt on a slug. Pour the mixture through a sieve to separate pumpkin and syrup. Collect the syrup in a large Pyrex mixing bowl.

Place the Pyrex bowl full of syrup in the microwave on high, and cook it until it boils up. As soon as it boils vigorously, open the door, and add the pumpkin to the syrup, and crank up the microwave again until the syrup boils up around the pumpkin for about 10 - 15 minutes Pumpkin should be barely fork tender. Remove from the microwave, and again pour the mixture through a sieve to separate pumpkin and syrup. Collect the syrup in the same Pyrex mixing bowl and set the pumpkin aside.

Return the Pyrex bowl full of only syrup to the microwave and boil it hard, watching it to prevent it from bubbling over the top of the mixing bowl. Also, don't overcook it. It should not be caramelized in the least. Each time you boil the syrup, expect your syrup to foam up nicely in the Pyrex bowl into a mound of clear frothy bubbles. Cook the syrup by itself until it is the consistency of pancake syrup. If you have a candy thermometer, it should be "string stage" about 230-235 degrees. When the syrup is reduced to that point, take it out and let it cool.

When cool, add back the pumpkin and allow the slices to sit in the syrup for another 4-6 hours, or overnight at room temp. Cover the bowl with a clean kitchen towel (not plastic wrap!). This should finish extracting most of the water from the fruit. This thins down your syrup again as more water is extracted from the fruit again. The pumpkin is now well on the way to being candied into mostarda. Your pumpkin strips should be very shrunken in size compared to their original size.

Finally, again pour the mixture through a sieve to separate the pumpkin and syrup. Collect the syrup in the same large Pyrex mixing bowl. And put syrup by itself back in the microwave for the last cooking. Boil it to the same "string stage" of 230-235 degrees, just about the thickness of pancake syrup again. Take it out of the microwave and allow the syrup to cool fully.

Pour the cooled syrup back over the pumpkin again.

Mix the mustard in with the white wine to form a thin paste and then pour all of this mustard paste into the pumpkin stirring completely to mix. Make sure to use a high grade of very fine dry mustard powder with lots of bite. Coleman's English Mustard is the standard in this category.

Put the mostarda into jars and seal. Normally mostarda is not hot processed like a canned item. It is just packed in jars. The sugar content is so high that it is not susceptible to spoilage, but you can keep it in a cool place or the refrigerator if you like.

If I Killed a Deer

Desserts

Pears Poached in Red Wine

Ingredients:

3 firm pears

¼ cup sugar

¼ cup water

1½ cup red table wine

3 - 4 whole black peppercorns

1 stick cinnamon

Directions:

Combine the spices, water, and wine, and bring to a boil in a stainless saucepan. Cook for about 15 minutes to obtain the spice flavor in the wine syrup. Peel the pears, and halve them lengthwise. Place the pear halves flat side down in a single layer in a pot large enough to hold all 6 halves. Pour the hot syrup over the pears, cover, and quickly bring the syrup to a simmer, and cook for no more than 5-10 minutes, depending on the ripeness of the pears. Do not overcook, or the pears will be mushy.

While still hot, use a spatula to transfer the pears from the pot into a round deep dish large enough to hold them in a single layer. Arrange in a circle with the stem ends toward the center, and the large ends out toward the outside of the circular dish. Continue to reduce the wine syrup down by boiling for another 10 minutes until it is about half the volume, then pour it over the poached pear halves. As you are pouring the syrup over the pears, strain it to remove the whole spices.

Allow the pears to cool, absorbing the syrup. Serve plain or with a scoop of ice cream.

Apple Honey Cake
Lekach

Ingredients:

2 large eggs-beaten

⅓ cup canola oil

½ tsp. ginger

Pinch ground cloves

1 tbsp. brandy, rum or whiskey

1 cup granulated sugar or brown sugar

¼ cup leftover strong black coffee (or tea)

3 large peeled cooking apples grated finely (1½ c. packed)

2 tsp. baking powder (Rumford non-aluminum)

2 cups flour

½ cup honey

1 tsp. cinnamon

½ tsp. salt

½ cup raisins (optional)

Directions:

Preheat oven to 325 degrees. Grease and flour a 9" x 5" rectangular loaf pan or tube pan (Bundt). Combine all of the dry ingredients except sugar and shake to blend in a Ziploc bag. Combine the coffee (tea) and honey and stir to dissolve the honey. Add the oil and brandy, and stir. Set aside. Beat the eggs and sugar together until well blended and fluffy. Combine the egg mixture with the coffee/honey mixture and stir to blend well. Add the grated apples and blend. Mix the dry ingredients to the mixing bowl containing the liquid ingredients in several parts, and then turn the batter out into the baking pan. Bake in oven for 40 - 45 minutes or until a toothpick comes out clean.

Lekach (Gluten Free Option):

Make a gluten free baking flour mix w. ¾ cup white rice flour, ½ cup potato starch, ¼ cup tapioca starch, ½ cup sorghum (or millet) flour, and 1 tsp. guar gum (or xanthan gum). Gluten free flours indicated here are made by Bob's Red Mill, and are sold extensively now.

Lekach (Carrot Option):

Substitute 1½ cups finely grated carrots
to the batter instead of the grated apples above.

Blackberry Jam Cake

I am including this recipe in memory of my grandmother, Harriet Buchanan Mullin who was raised in Abbs Valley, Tazewell, County, Virginia. Grandmother Mullin was a tiny lady who was quick as a wink in the kitchen. She could whip up a meal from scratch faster than anyone I have ever seen. Blackberry Jam Cake was one of her desserts my dad recalls as a boy in the coalfield town of Pocahontas, VA in the 1930's. This recipe is from a 1947 cookbook called **Favorite Recipes** *compiled by the Woman's Club of Bluefield, Virginia. This book's foreword says it is a successor to a previous book, the* **Victory Cookbook** *published during World War II. Bluefield, VA is only 9 miles from Pocahontas, VA, so it is likely this is the recipe that was popular in the coalfields at the time my dad was a boy. Although the recipe in the book does not call for it, my dad always called it Blackberry Jam Cake with Chocolate Icing. So, add some chocolate icing if you like.*

Ingredients:
1 cup sugar
1 cup blackberry jam
⅔ cup butter or ½ cup canola oil
½ cup buttermilk or sour milk
3 eggs
2 cups flour
2 tsp. baking powder (Rumford non-aluminum)
1 tsp. cinnamon
½ tsp. salt (if using unsalted butter)
⅛ tsp. cloves (optional)

Directions:
Combine all of the dry ingredients: flour, baking powder, & cinnamon in a Ziploc bag and shake to mix well. Mix the softened butter (or oil) and the sugar in a large mixing bowl with a whisk until smooth and creamy.

Beat the eggs and add them to the butter and sugar. Then add the jam, and mix well. Add the dry flour mixture, alternating with the buttermilk. Bake in a sheet cake pan at 350 degrees for about 25 - 30 minutes.

Gluten Free Option:

In place of the wheat flour, make a gluten free baking flour mix using ¾ cup white rice flour, ¾ cup potato starch, ¼ cup tapioca starch, ¼ cup sorghum (or millet) flour, and 1½ tsp. guar gum (or xanthan gum). Otherwise follow the directions above. Gluten free flours indicated here are made by Bob's Red Mill, and are sold extensively now in natural foods stores and some main line grocery stores.

Orange Polenta Cake
with Pecans & Ricotta

I first came across the notion of making a desert cake out of polenta (ground corn) when we were staying in Orvieto (Umbria) around Christmas 2007. We had a nice apartment near the cathedral, and did a lot of cooking. I made a polenta cake with ricotta cheese based on a recipe in a cookbook in the apartment. It seems these are quite popular in England, with all kinds of variations using orange, lemon, fruit preserves as toppings, etc. Use your imagination. Think of this as something like a dense pound cake.

Ingredients:

½ cup butter (unsalted)

1 cup sugar

1 cup fine ground yellow polenta or yellow corn meal

1 cup shelled pecans finely chopped

2 large eggs

2 tsp. vanilla extract

½ cup ricotta cheese

Juice of 2 oranges or ⅔ cup orange juice

Zest of orange

½ tsp salt

1 tsp. baking powder (Rumford non-aluminum)

Directions:

Preheat oven to 325 degrees. Grease or butter a 9-inch spring form pan. In a large bowl, beat the butter until light and creamy. Add sugar, and beat until fluffy. Add eggs, one at a time, mixing well after each addition. Mix in ricotta, vanilla, orange juice and zest.   Mix baking powder and salt with polenta and the ground pecans and fold all of the dry ingredients into the batter.   Pour into pan and bake for 40 - 45 minutes until golden and beginning to brown. Remove from oven and allow to cool. Cut into wedges and serve topped with fruit preserves or whipped cream.

Short-cut Pie Crust
with a Thin Dusted Crust

I seldom take time to make a real pie crust. It takes too much time! And, since I use rice flour because of my gluten intolerance, rolling a pie crust is a big pain anyway. This way makes a nice thin crust that you can prepare in a jiffy.

Ingredients:
½ stick butter
½ - ¾ cup flour or rice flour

Directions:
Soften the butter in a pie tin or Pyrex pie plate in oven or microwave. If in microwave, set on low, and cover to make sure it doesn't pop the butter and make a mess all over your microwave. Wrap your fingers in plastic wrap, and smear the butter on the entire inside of the pie plate so it is evenly covered. Pour flour in and rotate the pie plate, tapping it so the butter gets covered evenly by the flour. Any excess flour that won't stick to the layer of butter, just tip pie plate and discard that loose flour. This crust is not substantial enough for fruit pies like apple pie, or for meat pies.

African Spice Pie
Vinegar Pie

This is a type of chess pie.

Ingredients:

9 inch pie shell (or Thin Dusted Crust above)
1½ cups sugar
½ cup evaporated milk or buttermilk
1 tsp. vanilla extract

4 large eggs
2 tbsp. fine cornmeal or flour
¼ cup melted butter
3 tbsp. vinegar

Directions:
Cream together the eggs & sugar in a mixing bowl. Add the butter, buttermilk, cornmeal, vanilla, and vinegar. Pour into pie shell and bake in preheated 350 degree oven until set (about 45 min.)

Sweet Potato Pie
with Pecan Praline Topping

Ingredients:

9 inch pie shell

Filling:

3 large slow baked sweet potatoes 1 hour at 350 degrees

2 large eggs

1 cup sugar

¼ cup melted butter

½ tsp. cinnamon

¼ tsp. nutmeg

¾ cup evaporated (PET or Carnation) milk

Pecan Praline Topping:

½ cup brown sugar

4 tbsp. white or brown corn syrup

2 tbsp. butter

1 tsp. vanilla extract

1 cup chopped pecans

Directions:

Preheat oven to 350 degrees. Cream together the eggs, sugar, butter, & spices. Scoop the sweet potato out of the skins, and mash well with a fork on a plate. Add evaporated milk, and mix all ingredients together and whip thoroughly with a whisk. Pour into pie shell and bake about 40 minutes or until the custard filling is just set. Remove from oven & cool.

Meanwhile, combine all topping ingredients in a saucepan and heat to melt butter and allow topping to foam up once. Remove from heat, and spoon mixture onto the center of the sweet potato pie. Spread it out evenly on the surface.

If desired a meringue can be made and spoonfuls of meringue placed in a decorative pattern on top of the pie before returning to the oven.

Meringue (Optional):

2 egg whites and 4 tbsp. sugar. Pinch salt & ⅛ tsp. cream of tartar. Whip briskly in a very clean dry stainless mixing bowl until meringue develops stiff peaks. Dot top of pie with meringue dollops. Return to oven for 10-15 minutes more on 350 degrees to brown meringue.

Mary Baber Ellett's Baked Rice Custard

Ingredients:

2 large eggs plus 1 egg yolk

2¼ cups whole milk

¾ cup cooked rice (preferably short grain)

Scant ½ cup sugar

Handful of raisins

¼ Tsp. salt

1 tsp. vanilla extract

Sprinkle top with nutmeg, mace or cinnamon (optional)

Directions:

Preheat oven to 325 degrees. Beat eggs thoroughly with the sugar. Add vanilla & salt & mix. Select a shallow earthen casserole, preferably one of a dark color (the light color of this custard looks good in a brown glazed casserole). Spread the cooked rice evenly on bottom of the casserole. Then, sprinkle raisins evenly on top of the thin layer of rice. Gently pour the liquid over the rice and raisins and put in oven. Bake for approximately 50 minutes or until custard is slightly set. Don't overcook. It should still jiggle in the middle of the casserole, but not slosh when you lightly tap the dish in the oven. Cool on a rack to let air circulate below the dish. Serve warm or good for a few days refrigerated especially with sliced fresh strawberries or peaches.

Options:

1. Soak raisins in enough brandy to cover for 30 minutes before using.

2. Sprinkle top of custard with nutmeg or mace before baking.

3. Instead of nutmeg, add the zest of half a lemon to the dish for a Portuguese flavored rice pudding.

4. Sprinkle bottom of casserole dish evenly with a couple tablespoons of sugar and run it under the broiler long enough to caramelize, but don't burn the sugar. Then put your rice and raisins in, and proceed as above. This will give you a beautiful brown bottom with lots of delicious flavor like an upside down rice crème brûlée.

5. Non-dairy version: Substitute 2¼ cups of plain or vanilla rice milk for the cow's milk. Add 2 tsp. of corn starch or tapioca starch to the egg & milk. Mix thoroughly before pouring over the rice and raisins.

CPSIA information can be obtained at www.ICGtesting.com
Printed in the USA
LVOW130802111112

306780LV00001B/94/P